THE AUTHOR

Dorothy H. Jenkins, formerly garden editor of **The New York Times**, is very likely the most widely read writer on gardening in the whole country.

Born in Pennsylvania and a graduate of Mount Holyoke College, she started her career as an instructor at the Brooklyn Botanic Gardens. She lives in Connecticut where, as a firm believer in the practical, do-it-yourself method of gardening, she grows and tests roses on her own two acres. She has written half-a-dozen books on how to garden, including one for children.

Bantam Books is proud to bring you THE COMPLETE BOOK OF ROSES, a simple, comprehensive, do-it-yourself book on roses and their delights by an outstanding authority on practical gardening.

THE
COMPLETE BOOK
OF
ROSES

BY DOROTHY H. JENKINS

BANTAM HOME OWNER'S LIBRARY
TORONTO / NEW YORK / LONDON

THE COMPLETE BOOK OF ROSES

A Bantam Book / published January 1956
2nd printing ...... January 1956
3rd printing ...... January 1957
4th printing .... March 1960
5th printing .... March 1960
6th printing .... April 1961
7th printing .... December 1962
Bantam Home Owner's Library edition published March 1965
9th printing
10th printing

Cover photograph by Robert J. Martin from Shostal.

Library of Congress Catalog Card Number: 56-5937

All rights reserved.
© Copyright, 1956, by Dorothy H. Jenkins.

Published simultaneously in the United States and Canada.

PRINTED IN THE UNITED STATES OF AMERICA

Table of Contents

The Complete Book of

Roses

Chapter I

What Is a Rose?

THERE'S something about a rose. Whether it's pink, red, yellow or white, it adds distinction to the man or woman who wears one in a buttonhole. Distinction is brought to the room graced by a bouquet of cut roses, just as it is to the property where even one climber flaunts its blossoms over the doorway, or a miniature blooms in a crevice of the steps.

Everyone loves a rose, and few gardens or few properties lack this favorite of all flowers. It does not matter whether the garden is in Louisiana or Texas, New Hampshire or New Mexico, Illinois or Nevada, roses will bloom every year. And, what is more, they will bloom year after year, for most kinds of roses are long-lived and sturdy.

Few people, however, buy a rosebush as an investment. They buy it to enjoy its blooms—its rich coloring, satiny texture and, above all, fragrance. These are irresistible qualities that lead a new property owner to make one of his first purchases a rosebush. The man of the house may have his mind on grass seed, so that his lawn will look as good as his neighbor's, but the lady of the house is almost certain to want a rosebush. In this she is doing only what generations of homemakers have done before her. The pioneers who crossed the plains in Conestoga wagons carried with them slips of roses and their June companion, peonies, as hundreds of Father Hugo and Austrian Copper roses and Festiva maxima peonies blooming today in Colorado testify. And probably there were even a few rose slips carefully tended on the *Mayflower* or one of the ships that came soon after to the shores of this new country.

Roses are as well known and as well loved in Europe as they are in America. There, too, rosebushes of one kind or another have bloomed in dooryards for centuries. The rose was prized by the Greeks and the Romans and the Persians of long ago. Roses were supposed to have grown in the garden of Midas, and the Island of Rhodes was named for this flower. Roses marked the coins of this island, and even today they are woven into a garland on some of England's coins.

Roses early became a commodity of trade. Not only did the Romans make extravagant use of flowers and petals to strew tables, couches and even the streets, but the English during the Elizabethan era used dried rose petals for their scent in so many ways that they imported them from as far away as Constantinople. In the countries of southeastern Europe petals have been gathered for centuries to obtain attar of roses, a highly fragrant essential oil. Rosa alba and R. damascena, particularly variety Kazanlik, were the chief sources, as they are still.

Roses were used in the design on stamps, too, and appear again and again in coats of arms. And the custom of tendering a rose in payment of rent for land originated in England in bygone days. Today that charming custom of rental payment is perpetuated every September by a rose nursery in this country. For Conard-Pyle, in West Grove, Pennsylvania, discovered when they bought additional land some years ago that the original deed had called for the payment of "one red rose yearly if demanded." That was the stipulation of William Penn when he deeded a parcel of land in 1731 to his grandson, also named William Penn.

Perhaps no greater tribute could be paid to the rose than to use it for everyday services such as rent, stamps and coins. Several countries have chosen the rose as a symbol, among them England, Poland, Iran, Turkey, Bulgaria, Czechoslovakia, Romania and Honduras. In the United States, bills were introduced in 1955 by Senator Margaret Chase Smith and Representative Frances Bolton to make the rose the national flower. Many people are heartily in favor of this; others believe the national flower should be one exclusively native to this country.

There are native, or species, roses that belong to this country only. One of them is the prairie rose (R. setigera) with deep pink single flowers, which is the official state flower of North Dakota. Iowa has chosen the wild rose, which might be any one of several species; New York, the rose; and Georgia, the lovely single white Cherokee rose which came originally from China or Japan.

Some roses are native to China and Japan, just as others are to Europe and North America, for roses grow all over the northern hemisphere. No one knows for sure how many species there are. Some say less than 100, some say 200, some say 4,000, and some say 4,000 in Eurasia alone. But it is doubtful if anyone, when he thinks of a rose, thinks of the single, five-petaled flower that opens on the native or wild bushes. Nowadays we usually think of roses as being fully double. Hybrid teas with eighty to 100 petals are not uncommon, and many modern varieties have thirty-odd petals, seldom less.

However many petals the flower has, it grows on a prickly shrub or vine. The leaves appear alternately along the stems, and are compound, with one leaflet always at the tip. Flowers are either solitary or in clusters, and may be white, yellow, any of the innumerable tints or tones of pink or red, or blends or any two or three of these tints or tones, or bicolors (top of the petal one shade, underside a contrasting one). But there's no such thing as a true blue rose, and probably there never will be. There is, however, actually a green rose!

The urn-shaped seed pod of the rose is called a hip. However, except on certain climbers and shrub roses, on which especially decorative red hips develop, faded flowers are seldom left to form these seed pods, except by a hybridizer.

The gardeners and hybridizers, generation after generation of them, have crossed one species or variety of rose with another to give us more than 6,000 known and named varieties today (not all, of course, are currently in commerce). Some of these hybridizers are responsible for the fact that roses no longer bloom only in May and June. Roses which repeat their bloom are called remontant. Others really deserve the term everblooming, for once they begin in May or June they continue until frost.

There's no such thing any more as "the last rose of summer." In the warmer climates of Florida and California it's possible to pick a rose outdoors almost any day of the year. But even in New England, where frost may come in September, it is possible some years to pick in November a red Carrousel or a pink Dream Girl or Radiance.

Modern roses are long-blooming, but roses have always been long-lived. Bushes have tremendous vigor, for they may put forth three or five or even six sets of leaves in a single year. The first set may make a tentative appearance in a mild January, only to be frozen by more winter weather. Then bushes may be defoliated by a disease such as black spot in summer, but put out another set of leaves and bloom again in September. Some kinds of roses will live and flower, untended by anyone, for years. But modern ones, if the plants are given some attention once in a while during the growing season, bloom more nearly as their originators meant they should.

It is next to impossible to kill a rosebush, either with kindness or neglect. However much or little care is given to a single or a hundred bushes in a garden, it is repaid by the flowers. And when they open, no one disagrees with the poet who called the rose "queen of the garden."

Chapter II

Hybrid Tea Roses

IF SOMEONE asked what a rose looked like, the reply, nine times out of ten, would be a description of a hybrid tea. Hybrid tea roses are the aristocrats of the family, and they are the darlings, though sometimes spoiled and pampered, of twentieth-century gardens.

For the last fifty or more years everyone has been growing hybrid tea roses. Special varieties that do well under glass and can be forced into bloom out of season have been developed for the cut-flower business. By far the greatest number of some 3,000 to 4,000 varieties have been originated for outdoor planting. They glorify public parks, municipal rose gardens and neighborhood gardens everywhere.

"The favorite class of rose in Northwest gardens is the hybrid tea, doubtless because it is such a fine exhibition type as well as being beautiful in the garden and as a cut flower," says Drew Sherrard, garden editor of the Portland *Oregonian*. Her statement is as applicable to the Northeast, where weather is more rugged—neighbors of mine, just average suburban gardeners, still have many of the hybrid tea bushes that they planted twenty-five years ago—and to balmy Florida, where hybrid teas bloom so constantly that bushes are exhausted after a year and must be replaced.

Everyone loves the bloom of a hybrid tea. The flowers are elegant and beautiful. They are gloriously pictured in rose nurserymen's catalogues—large flowers, petals half unfurled, richly colored. It's a rare person who can look at these pages and not yearn to cut one in his own garden just like the one in the picture. And the truth is that he can.

A good hybrid tea rose might be summed up as a nice big rose with petals of good substance, pleasing fragrance and a firm stem, and, because of all these qualities, a rose exceed-ingly good for cutting. Hybrid teas in the temperate zone have their big burst of bloom in June (some may start in May), flower recurrently all summer, and have a second, more richly colored display again in September. Thereafter they bloom intermittently until the buds freeze.

In sunny California, May is considered the month of roses, but bloom there from hybrid teas throughout the summer is at least 50 per cent heavier than in other parts of the country. Flowering is constant from March to November—and indeed some roses, if not hybrid teas, bloom every month of the year.

Bushes of hybrid teas grow fifteen inches to four feet tall and need no support. The average height is about three feet. Every bush has several main stems, or canes. Some varieties are quite spreading in their habit of growth, others are fairly upright.

The characteristics of plant and flower that make a hybrid tea are the product of its parentage—the tea rose brought to Europe from India and China, and the hybrid perpetual. Credit for the first hybrid tea rose goes to Guillot in France, although breeding along similar lines for the same type of flower was going on simultaneously in France and England. This first hybrid tea in 1861 was named, appropriately, La France. Its blossoms have about sixty petals, somewhat curled, bright pink with silvery tints and intensely fragrant. La France is still listed in a large number of catalogues, while many hybrid tea varieties introduced as recently as ten years ago have already been dropped from the lists.

Since La France was first recognized in 1867, European and English hybridizers have produced one new variety after another. Soon after 1900 hybridizers in this country started adding to the lists. New varieties, each with some distinctive difference from all its predecessors, continue to be introduced annually. In some years there may be only one or two new ones; then again there may be a dozen, with as many as four from a single American nursery.

Most often the differences are in the flower itself. A hybrid tea may average as few as twenty to thirty petals, as in the modern pink First Love or old Red Radiance; thirty to forty petals, as in crimson Charles Mallerin; forty to fifty, as in bright crimson Chrysler Imperial or rose and mauve Miss Rowena Thom. The greater the number of petals, the larger the open flower, of course.

Buds may be round and blunt, or long and pointed. The yellow Eclipse is noted for its exceptionally long, pointed and handsome bud; the flower actually is somewhat of a letdown. On the other hand, Diamond Jubilee has rather scrubby-

Ovoid

Globular

Pointed

Slender

Urn

FORMS OF BUDS

7

looking fat round buds which open to double flowers of an
exquisite yellow-buff tone. Beautiful long and tapered buds
are typical of varieties introduced by at least one American
nursery, Armstrong of California, for the founder insists on
this. Among their introductions with buds characteristically
as beautiful as the flowers are Charlotte Armstrong, Sutter's
Gold and First Love.

There is variation in flower form, too. Probably the majority of hybrid teas are fairly high-centered and may not
even show stamens when fully open. This gives the effect of
a deep flower. But there are some that open as round roses.
Radiance is one of these, and probably no hybrid tea is more
perfectly globose than the shell-pink Mrs. Charles Bell. A few
hybrid teas open as almost flat, many-petaled blooms, remi-
niscent of the old-fashioned cabbage and moss roses. The red
President Eisenhower, when fully open, has somewhat this
petal arrangement, although buds are pointed, long and plump.

Far more often than size or shape, color is the reason for
naming and introducing a new variety. This may be some
fresh tint, tone or gradation, or even a fresh combination
of color. Bicolor or two-toned contrasts and blends have been
exceedingly popular in recent years. So we now have Forty-
Niner with the inside of the petals vivid red, the outside straw
color; Saturnia, cardinal red with yellow reverse; and brilliant
blends such as Mojave's salmon, apricot and orange, and
Comtesse Vandal, pink suffused with yellow. Talisman, a
brilliant blend of red and gold introduced in 1929, promptly
became a favorite. Developed by the Montgomery Company
in Massachusetts, it does best under glass. Far more satisfactory outdoors is Condesa de Sastago, originated by Pedro Dot
in Spain a few years later. Condesa is a two-toned red and
gold rather than a blend of colors.

A distinctive color break came with Grey Pearl, introduced
in 1944. A blending of tan and olive turning to lavender gray
is characteristic of its small flowers. On the whole, the odd
shading has probably appealed more to those who make a
cult of flower arrangement rather than to the amateur rose
grower. Then in 1955 came Twilight, with larger flowers that
are lavender with a silvery lilac reverse.

Good yellows in the hybrid tea class are the result of complicated crossbreeding by a French hybridist, J. Pernet-
Ducher. Once called the Pernetiana type, his roses now are
included in the hybrid tea group.

But there have been other valid reasons than color for the
development of new varieties and strains. Recently in this
country Mr. and Mrs. Walter Brownell in Rhode Island
brought about a group which they call sub-zero hybrid teas.

In other words, the Brownells' aim has been to produce a hardier hybrid tea rose. In almost every case I have found the bushes tend to be massive in growth. Nevertheless such varieties as coppery Ann Vanderbilt are truly handsome.

Between 1914 and 1925 half a dozen charming single hybrid teas were introduced. Best known is six-petaled Dainty Bess, with dark stamens against its delicate pink petals. Newer and equally lovely is the five-petaled White Wings, also accented by its wine-colored stamens. Lulu should be better known for its beautiful long buds if not its coppery pink flowers. There are also crimson Vesuvius, coppery red Irish Fireflame, orange-pink Isobel, yellow Cecil and twelve-petaled white Innocence.

At the other extreme is the big double Peace. A nine-year-old girl who is enchanted with all animals and flowers told me that her favorite flower in the garden is Peace—not just a rose, but Peace rose. Her choice is unerring, for Peace has topped the American Rose Society's annual poll of favorite roses so often that it has been tagged "the most popular rose of the era."

In spite of its size, which is undoubtedly a factor in its popularity, Peace is a rose of delicacy, borne on strong stems with glossy foliage. Part of its fascination is its coloring—golden buds opening to creamy gold flowers flushed with pink at the edge of the petals—the pink deepening each day of the rose's life. Originated by Francis Meilland in France, Peace was introduced to this country by an American nurseryman in 1945. It won an All-America Award for 1946.

Peace represents a milestone in hybrid tea history. Other varieties of significance include Radiance, an excellent pink bred by John Cook of Baltimore and introduced in 1908; salmon Los Angeles, originated by Fred Howard in California, which in 1916 was the first American-bred hybrid tea to win an award at the oldest test garden, La Roserie de la Haye in Paris; and Etoile de Hollande, long a standard of dark red and fragrance. Salmon Ophelia (1912) and rosy red Charlotte Armstrong (1941) are famous not only as splendid garden roses but also as good parents of an increasing number of fine hybrid teas.

Fragrance is a variable quality. Probably none exceeds and few equal that of the old La France and modern Crimson Glory. There are many types of rose fragrance—the rich scent of Crimson Glory, the spiciness of Helen Traubel, the fruity odor of pink Katherine T. Marshall, the slight tea fragrance of pink Mission Bells, the old damask smell of red Christopher Stone and the just plain sweetness of Pink Dawn.

Form, color and fragrance add up to beauty in a rose. But

new varieties do not win a following on beauty alone. They must be hardy over the larger part of the country; they must be vigorous and strong-growing. Roses that lack these qualities soon drop out of the catalogue listings. Some degree of resistance to common diseases of the rose is desirable and is included in current hybridizing aims.

No matter how continuously a hybrid tea blooms or how vigorously it grows between spring and fall each year, it requires regular attention. It is true that a hybrid tea rose can be planted in winter or spring, depending on the part of the country, with confidence that it will flower that year. It will, certainly, within three to four months. And depending on the variety, it may continue to bloom quite creditably for several years, even if neglected.

However, there does not seem to be much point to growing a rose unless it produces flowers that look the way they ought to look. In order to do this, every hybrid tea requires understanding pruning annually and faithful spraying throughout its growing season. It's possible to learn how to prune (Chapter XII). And anyone can spray (Chapter XI). The important point is that spraying must be done not less often than every ten days and preferably once a week while roses are in leaf. Spraying must be done wherever hybrid teas are grown, for every part of the country has specific diseases and insects that attack the hybrid tea varieties.

More vigorous in their growth than the hybrid teas are their immediate predecessors, hybrid perpetual roses. Their heyday was the last quarter of the nineteenth century. The first hybrid perpetual, a blending of several species, appeared in 1837. It and its successors proved immensely popular until about 1890, when hybrid teas began appearing in greater number.

Many a garden today still includes at least one hybrid perpetual, and for good reason. That one is the handsome white Frau Karl Druschki, whose only possible drawback is lack of fragrance. The plants, however, are both hardier and thriftier than most of the white hybrid tea varieties.

Another hybrid perpetual that many a knowing gardener refuses to do without is General Jacqueminot. Intense fragrance is the reason, and also, perhaps, its clear red petals. I must admit that I would never be without hybrid perpetual Mrs. R. G. Sharmon-Crawford, a charming, clear, light pink rose. Mrs. Crawford blooms for me even more profusely than Frau Karl Druschki.

The hybrid perpetuals' habit of bloom is one good reason why they have been superseded by the hybrid teas. Hybrid perpetuals are classed as recurrent blooming. That is, they

flower heavily in June and lightly about once a month thereafter through the season.

Any hybrid perpetual grows four to six feet tall each year.
Its canes are strong and vigorous, upright and straight—they
make big, tall plants.

Probably every rose catalogue still lists two or three hybrid
perpetuals, and a few carry a dozen or more. Among varieties
still worth considering are:

> Frau Karl Druschki—*white*
> General Jacqueminot—*red*
> Mrs. R. G. Sharmon-Crawford—*pink*
> Paul Neyron—*lilac pink*
> Ulrich Brunner—*cherry red*

Varieties of hybrid tea roses vary in hardiness and popularity in different parts of the country. In the Northwest, for
example, Ena Harkness ranks with Crimson Glory among
dark reds. In the East, Ena Harkness is little known.

In some regions, too, there may be a vast difference in the
performance of a variety being grown in places only a few
miles apart. This is especially true in California, where a
certain variety of red hybrid tea may bloom magnificently
along the coast, while in an inland valley less than fifty miles
away it may be utterly unsatisfactory and another red variety reign supreme instead.

Yet hybrid teas are the great favorites. In fact, again referring to California, specifically the Palo Alto area, hybrid tea
varieties are considered better performers, even in summer,
than the floribundas, which are generally sturdier elsewhere.

The following varieties, according to color, are thrifty
enough to be planted confidently north, south, east or west:

Red	*White*
Christian Dior	Blanche Mallerin
Crimson Glory	Pedrables
Etoile de Hollande	Sincera
Grand Slam	Virgo
Mister Lincoln	White Knight

Light Pink	*Deep or Rose Pink*
Confidence	Charlotte Armstrong
First Love	Picture
Radiance	Pink Peace
Royal Highness	Show Girl
Tiffany	The Doctor

Yellow

Eclipse—deep yellow, noted for beautiful bud

King's Ransom—canary yellow

Lowell Thomas—chrome yellow

Soeur Therese—buttercup yellow

Summer Sunshine—rich yellow, colorfast

Orange

Aztec—orange scarlet

Hawaii—orange coral

Orange Flame—orange scarlet to smoky orange

Tropicana—orange red

Bicolor

Condesa de Sastago—copper inside, gold reverse

Forty-Niner—vivid red inside, straw color reverse

Kordes Perfecta—creamy white and carmine petals

Suspense—red inside, yellow outside

Traviata—each petal red and white

Blends

Chicago Peace—more brilliant and fragrant than Peace

Helen Traubel—pink and apricot

Mojave—orange with vermilion

Peace—shades of yellow and pink

Sutter's Gold—gold shaded with red

Lavender

Lavender Charm—deep lavender

Simone—lilac lavender

Sterling Silver—lavender, faintly pink when open

Chapter III

Climbing Roses

THERE probably is not a town or a city anywhere in this country where at least one yard doesn't have a climbing rose. Come June, every climber everywhere is loaded with blossoms and, depending on where the town or city is, some climbers bloom from March to December.

On St. Patrick's Day every year in southern California the fragrant white Banksia is flowering. By Easter in South Carolina the lovely pink blossoms of Cherokee are wafting their sweetness through the air. By Memorial Day all of New Jersey is afire with the blooms of Paul's Scarlet and Blaze. Fourth of July travelers on the New York, New Haven and Hartford Railroad through New England are delighted with the little double blossoms of Crimson Rambler and pink Dorothy Perkins thriving in the cinders. And by mid-July the Island of Nantucket is a tangle of climbing roses in full bloom.

These roses may drape their length along rustic fences, hang over walls, clamber over roadside embankments, transform a clothespole, glorify an arbor, festoon a porch. But whether they scramble over the ground or lean against a post, climbing roses open their flowers to the sun and silhouette them against the sky, in late spring and on through the summer and autumn.

Strangely enough, climbing roses do not actually climb. Unlike true vines, such as clematis, which pulls itself up by curling tendrils, and Boston ivy, with aerial discs or roots, a climbing rose has no means of fastening itself to a support except its thorns. And whatever purpose thorns do or do not serve, they certainly do not help a rose to climb. Climbing roses, therefore, are actually extraordinarily tall-growing plants. The canes of all varieties average not less than eight

13

to ten feet tall, and are too flexible to hold that height erect.
These tall roses are given the appearance of being a climber
by tying their canes to some sort of support. Left to themselves, the plants would only sprawl or clamber over the
ground.

Abundance is the synonym for climbing roses in bloom.
So luxuriant is an established plant that nobody who buys a
new one expects failure. Indeed, failure is the exception, and
can always be traced to some specific cause. This much should
be remembered: It takes two years for a climbing rose to
show what it's really like and what it can do. Unlike the hybrid
teas and floribundas, which produce blooms of quality and in
profusion three months after being planted, the climbers take
two full years, although they may have a modest flower display the first summer.

After the second year, the climbers seem to go on forever.
Climbing roses are both vigorous and hardy. Of course there
are some, such as Banksia and Cherokee, that live from year
to year only in mild climate. And the lovely single white
Mermaid is not considered reliably hardy north of Philadelphia. There was a time—some twenty-five or more years ago
—when there were no yellow-flowering climbers rugged
enough to withstand the winter of the Northeast and Middle
Atlantic States without ample bundling up. But all that has
changed. Now there are not only vigorous but hardy climbers
in each of the rose colors that will live through many winters
and flower for many summers, no matter what the prevailing
climate.

Climbers can be classified according to their habit of
growth. Some that have six to eight feet as their maximum
height are often called pillar roses because, obviously, their
height makes them most suitable for growing against some
sort of post. There is a group of trailing or creeping roses
whose very long canes are suitable only for trailing along the
ground. Planted where they can hang down over a wall or
boulder, they are graceful, but they just aren't right espaliered
up against a high wall or a building.

But, of course, the flowers rather than the plants are always
the reason for planting roses. And climbing roses subdivide
naturally into three main groups, according to the size and
form of the flowers. This also is the way most catalogues list
climbers. There are large-flowered climbers, ramblers, and
climbing hybrid teas.

The large-flowered climbers have blooms that are comparable to a medium-sized hybrid tea rose on a bush. The
blooms may be single as in Silver Moon and Mermaid, or
double as in Dream Girl, New Dawn or High Noon.

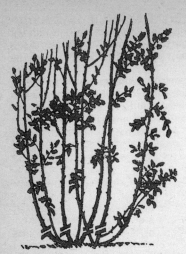

Pruning ramblers—after bloom, cut off at
ground level all canes which have flowered

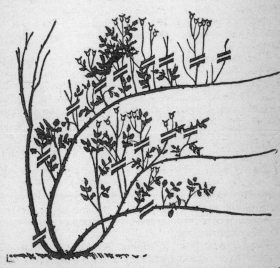

Pruning large-flowered climbers—after bloom, cut off
side shoots. If desired, main stems may be shortened

Most of the new climbing roses—and it's a rare year when there aren't one or more new ones—are large-flowering climbers. Perhaps that is why most people think of this group as being the most modern, but actually some of the standard varieties date back forty to fifty years. Paul's Scarlet appeared in 1916, Silver Moon and Dr. W. Van Fleet in 1910.

One or perhaps two characteristics of many varieties reflect modern demands of roses. One is the ability to be either remontant or everblooming; the other is fragrance. Old roses have always been noted for their fragrance. Then for a time this quality was neglected. Already fragrance is notable in such recent varieties as Dream Girl and Coral Dawn, and may be expected more consistently in introductions to come.

The ability to bloom not only in June but either periodically or regularly throughout the summer first came with New Dawn in 1930. This is a sport of the lovely delicate pink Dr. W. Van Fleet. Blaze, which came out in 1932, is the everblooming counterpart of Paul's Scarlet. Now no large-flowered climber is introduced unless it is everblooming.

Everblooming is a term that is perhaps more promising than true. Climbing roses never again during the year equal the quantity of bloom that opens in June. Then suddenly in early July the plants are bare except for their green foliage. By the end of that month a few new flowers may open, and they will continue to bloom intermittently until fall, when another sizable burst of bloom appears.

Everblooming varieties vary in the constancy and quantity of their bloom. And no climbing rose, however consistent it may be in later years, will be everblooming the first summer it is in the garden. In my Connecticut garden Dream Girl has proved more worthy of the term "everblooming" than has Pink Cloud or New Dawn. Dr. J. H. Nicolas, an enormous pink, is admitted in catalogues to be remontant rather then everblooming.

Swelling the number of everblooming climbers are the climbing hybrid tea and floribunda roses. Climbing Goldilocks, climbing Pinkie and climbing Summer Snow have flowers that are identical to the floribunda bush roses with the same names. Both bush and climbing forms flower steadily all summer and into fall.

Climbing hybrid teas will bear flowers of the same size and of the same frequency as the bush hybrid tea of the same name. Climbing Crimson Glory is one of the most generous. If the yellow Lowell Thomas, pink Picture and McGredy's Ivory do well as bush hybrid teas, then a climber of the same name is worth trying in the same garden. Climbing hybrid teas are a staple in southern California and other parts of the Southwest and in the Southeast. In southern Connecticut I do grow climbing floribundas such as Goldilocks, but I do not grow climbing hybrid teas, although I know people in the northern part of the state who do.

Climbing hybrid teas can be grown successfully in the Northeast and carried over from year to year, but they are more work than other kinds of climbers. From Washington, D. C., northward and westward, wherever winters are cold or likely to have fluctuations of temperature, climbing hybrid teas must be given ample protection. And this takes much more time and trouble than providing adequate winter protection for bush hybrid teas (page 83). With or without protection, there may be some years when some of the canes will be winterkilled entirely, or for part of their length. This means a longer wait for profuse bloom, because canes will have to make new growth.

But modern rambler roses are no trouble, winter or summer, to anyone anywhere. These plants have long flexible canes tipped with clusters of small flowers, seldom more than an inch in diameter. They are as pretty as can be, but they bloom only once a year—in late June and early July, following the first flowering of the large-flowered climbers. On the other hand, ramblers are strong-growing and thrifty, dependable year after year.

The two standard varieties are the Crimson Rambler, introduced in 1893, and pink Dorothy Perkins, dating back to 1901. Everyone knows these two, just from seeing them grow so commonly around the country. Those that bloom along the New York, New Haven and Hartford Railroad tracks were planted in the twenties, and without any attention bloom without fail every June or July.

Nevertheless modern gardeners are better off choosing more modern varieties to plant. That is because Crimson Rambler and Dorothy Perkins are subject to mildew, a disease that coats buds and stems with gray mold. They bloom in spite of this, but are unsightly in the years when weather favors the development of mildew.

Less susceptible to this disease are all the newer ramblers and some of the old ones. Crimson Chevy Chase and rosy crimson Excelsa are big improvements over Crimson Rambler. Pink Minnehaha, yellow Brownell Rambler and Sanders' White Rambler are healthy as well as reliable.

White rambler roses do well at covering and holding a bank, there is a group of typical trailing or creeping roses that is especially suited to this purpose. They are perfect as groundcover for slopes, to foam over a boulder or create a colorful cascade over a wall. The classic trailing rose is Max Graf, with handsome disease-resistant foliage somewhat like that of the shrubbery Rugosa roses, and single blossoms three inches across in exquisite pink with clusters of golden stamens. This hybrid variety needs no care and will flower even in part shade.

A sheaf of varieties has been added to the trailing or creeping group in recent years by Mr. and Mrs. Walter Brownell of Little Compton, Rhode Island. They should be saluted for the colors of these roses as well as for the vigor and hardiness of the plants. The foliage usually is glossy and handsome. My favorite of all the Brownell varieties is Little Compton Creeper, with large single flowers of true pink. Large bright red hips are colorful in autumn and early winter.

Coral Creeper has deep red buds opening to semi-double coral flowers. Carpet of Gold has double yellow flowers; Magic Carpet, a mixture of yellow and orange blossoms.

In mild climates the Banksia and Cherokee roses lend themselves fully as successfully to trailing as to climbing use. And climbers, like all other classes of roses, in mild climates start to bloom earlier in the year and continue later. Elsewhere, although many of the climbers bloom only once early in the season, certain varieties may have a second color display in the fall from another source—the hips or seed pods in varying shades of red. If flowers are not snipped off after they fade, a display of hips follows on many varieties. Among those that add a real splash of color to the November landscape are Little Compton Creeper, rambler Bloomfield Courage, and the large-flowered climbers Dr. W. Van Fleet, American Pillar and Spanish Beauty.

The following lists are based on personal experience and observation and, in the case of the regional selections, on discussions with gardeners who live in those areas. Selections have been made for each basic color and type of climbing rose.

*Ramblers

Red	Bloomfield Courage
	Chevy Chase
Pink	Minnehaha
Yellow	Aviateur Blériot
	Brownell's Rambler
White	Sanders' White Rambler

* Displaced by longer-blooming, large-flowering climbers

Trailing

Yellow	Carpet of Gold
Pink	Coral Creeper
	Little Compton Creeper
	*Max Graf

Pillar

Red	*Don Juan
	*Pillar of Fire
Pink	Reichsprasident von Hindenburg
White	Morning Stars
	Prosperity
Yellow	Clytemnestra

Everblooming

Climbing hybrid teas and climbing floribundas automatically belong to this class. Varieties should be chosen to suit the climate. Large-flowering climbers that are everblooming are:

Red	Improved Blaze
	Red Empress
Pink	Blossomtime
	New Dawn
White	White Dawn
Yellow	Golden Showers

Large-Flowered Climbers

Northeastern, Middle Atlantic and Middlewestern States

Red	Gladiator
	**Improved Blaze
	**Lancaster
	**Red Empress
Pink	**Blossomtime
	**Claire Matin
	**Dr. J. H. Nicolas
White	**White Dawn
Yellow	**Golden Showers

* Generally available
** Everblooming or remontant

Southeastern States

Red	**Improved Blaze
	Cherokee
Pink	Mme. Gregoire Staechelin (Spanish Beauty)
	**New Dawn
White	Banksia
	**Mermaid (single)
Yellow	Banksia
	**Maréchal Niel

The Southwest

Red	**Improved Blaze
Pink	Belle Portugaise
	**Blossomtime
	Mme. Gregoire Staechelin (Spanish Beauty)
White	**White Dawn
Yellow	**Golden Showers
	**High Noon

The Northwest

Red	**Improved Blaze
Pink	**Blossomtime
	Pinkie
White	**White Dawn
Yellow	**Golden Showers
	**High Noon

Rocky Mountain States

Red	**Improved Blaze
Pink	**Blossomtime
	**New Dawn
White	**White Dawn
Yellow	**Golden Showers

** Everblooming or remontant

Chapter IV

Tree and Miniature Roses

THE ROSE is not an imitative flower, with blossoms of some varieties resembling a camellia, a geranium or a tuberous begonia. Whether the bloom is an inch wide or eight inches across when fully open, whether it has one row of petals or is bursting with so many that they can't be counted, a rose is always unmistakably a rose.

The inimitable rose, however, blooms on plants that grow in many different ways. Most generally seen is the bush rose, which has an average height of two to four feet. But there are shrubs which grow tall and broad, and plants that climb or ramble or trail or creep. And then there are the tree rose and the miniature rose.

A tree rose is for all the world a living bouquet, but one that exists in soil instead of water. Such a plant holds its bunch of flowers well above those of most other rosebushes in the garden. On the other hand, a miniature rose plant might be compared to a little nosegay, fresh as dew on a summer morning. Both the tree rose and the miniature rose make wonderful decorative accents.

A tree rose, sometimes called a standard rose, is valued for its height as well as for its manner of growth. Tree is the more descriptive term for, like a shade tree, the tree rose consists of a single main stem or trunk topped with a crown of short stems thick with foliage and flowers. Two, three or four feet is the usual height. No rose grows naturally in this manner. A tree rose is man-made by budding (see page 96) a hybrid tea, hybrid perpetual, floribunda, grandiflora or miniature on top of a straight stem. Sometimes this main stem is exceedingly thorny, sometimes it is a thick, straight and shining cane, depending on the type of rose preferred by the grower for the purpose.

A miniature rose is a natural plant, a perfect bush that could be covered by a pint measure, and has foliage and flowers in absolute scale to its over-all size. Most species and varieties of miniature roses average six to nine inches in height, although one or two do reach twelve inches. These bushes are seldom as broad as they are tall. The whole leaf (and remember, a true rose leaf consists of five leaflets, two pairs and a terminal, on a single stem) measures no more than two inches long, and the blossoms are no bigger than the tip of a person's little finger. A thimble would be the right size container for a bouquet of miniature roses.

Neither a tree rose nor a miniature rose is grown primarily to provide cut flowers. Both types are prolific of bloom. The miniatures start flowering in my Connecticut garden in May and continue into November. During this period it's a rare day when some, if not all, of the miniature roses don't have a little flower. In the Tyler, Texas, Municipal Rose Garden, the miniature Baby Gold Star set something of a record for 1954-1955. Bushes continued their 1954 flowering unbroken until February 10, 1955, and on March 19, 1955, had started another year of bloom.

Tree roses do not start to bloom much before June in the Northeast and similar areas where there are four distinct seasons, including a cold winter. Depending on the variety chosen for budding, bloom is either constant or intermittent from then until October. In mild climates the season of bloom begins about two months earlier and lasts six weeks to two months longer.

Why then are tree roses and miniature roses so popular? It must be because of their unusual habits of growth which result in such effective plantings.

Because of their size, the miniatures make it possible to grow roses in places where it would otherwise be impossible to enjoy this beloved flower. They are most appropriate for a rock garden and especially valuable there for bloom in summer, a sparse flowering period for run-of-the-mill rock garden plants. They are also suited to the low wall. My favorite spot for miniatures is in the crevices at the side of flagstone steps —a perfect setting. Being such low plants, miniatures also are good to edge beds of hybrid tea or floribunda roses—or, in fact, to be used almost any place that an edging plant is needed. They can be grown in strawberry jars, too, one plant in each pocket, for the porch or terrace in summer.

With tree roses, too, it's their height that determines where they will be planted. With their crowns of flowers, they are, above all, dramatic plants. Their height, particularly of the three- and four-foot ones, is invaluable for varying the expanse of a border or bed of bush roses. No other plant breaks up this level sea of rose bloom quite as effectively.

Perhaps even more effective are tree roses planted in pairs by themselves, or towering over plants other than roses. That narrow strip along the driveway from street to garage might be sown to sweet alyssum or planted with a green perennial groundcover such as sedum or Vinca minor, and then be planted with a line of tree roses, about six feet apart.

A pair of tree roses might be planted on either side of the entrance to the house or on either side of the entrance walk. A pair might mark and give importance to the entrance to the garden or to any garden path. Since they are primarily accent plants, tree roses in pairs or paired groups of three can be used to mark any entrance way, whether to garden, terrace or the property as a whole.

To fulfill their role of accent, tree roses should not be scattered haphazardly among other shrubs. If they are set out at intervals in front of a high fence or wall, their dramatic quality is emphasized.

The smallest size of tree rose, with a total height of two feet, is ideal for growing in tubs to be placed on the terrace or in the patio. This two-foot tree consists of a ten-inch cane supporting a twelve-inch crown which is one of the miniature roses. This little tree rose is common only in mild climates such as southern California where this group gives its best performance.

When they are growing in favorable climate, soil and location and are true bouquets of bloom, I can admire tree roses. (Miniature roses I would never be without.) But the areas in the United States where tree roses can manage to achieve this ideal growth and production of flowers are extremely limited. I have seen luxuriant tree roses in the summer in Greenwich, Connecticut, and Newark, New York, among other places in the Northeast. But these are the exception rather than the rule. Magnificent tree roses are seen on every hand in and about Los Angeles and other parts of southern California, and after seeing them there I don't even want to try to grow them in Connecticut. But other parts of the Southwest where climate is more rugged, such as New Mexico with its winds and very dry atmospheric conditions, prove to be not wholly satisfactory for the tree roses. They are best left for gardeners who live in mild southern climates, although with perseverance they can be grown anywhere.

A tree rose should only be planted with the most solemn promises to keep it always a thing of beauty. That means not only that blossoms should be cut off as fast as they fade, so that the tree will look neat, but also that blossoms and foliage should never be marred by disease or insects. To keep the plants healthy, then, is the gardener's main chore, wherever he lives. Feeding and cultivation parallel that for hybrid teas, but the finest growth in the long run results not so much from the gardener's regular attention as from the climate that is most favorable.

Incidentally, tree roses everywhere should always be tied in two or three places along the main cane, to a slender wooden or bamboo stake. This is support for the top load of bloom and for storms.

The real chore in all regions except the most southerly comes with winter protection. Tree roses are not notably hardy even if the hybrid tea or floribunda bloom on them is perfectly hardy when growing as a plant and not a tree. The trouble point is not the crown or the trunk but the point of union. In the large area where winter is either severe or a season of fluctuating temperatures, tree roses must be wrapped or otherwise protected where they are growing, or else dug up and buried (see page 86).

The person who is going to grow tree roses, in either favorable or unfavorable climate, buys primarily by color instead of variety. Every year tree roses are available in each of the standard rose colors, and production, which is more complicated than for a bush rose, is limited to a few of the popular varieties in each of these colors. In California it may be possible to choose among six to twelve varieties of red roses, including hybrid teas, floribundas, grandifloras and miniatures. In the East the choice is likely to be limited to four or perhaps six varieties in a color.

Miniatures are bought by name, and in recent years new varieties have been developed so that almost a complete rose color range is available. Hybridizing activity within the last twenty-five years or so, most of it centered in Holland, has either indicated or brought about another wave of popularity for the miniature roses. One such wave of popularity occurred early in the nineteenth century when the miniature was commonly known as Miss Lawrance's rose, or Rosa lawranciana, in honor of Mary Lawrance, flower portrait painter. This is just one of several names given to the rose listed botanically as R. chinensis minima. Another variation is Rosa rouletti, found in Switzerland and known almost as long as R. chinensis minima.

Rouletti is still listed in some catalogues. It has rose-pink double flowers an inch in diameter. Far more attractive, to my way of thinking, are the modern varieties. Sweet Fairy is adorable and sturdy. Its dark pink buds open to light pink, very double blossoms with a true, rich rose fragrance. It is both the most fragrant and perhaps most constant blooming miniature I have grown.

Pixie and Cinderella are white, and of the several reds, Red Imp might be described as a miniature Crimson Glory. Red Elf is darker. The only yellow, Baby Gold Star, grows all of two feet tall in Texas and Oregon, but much less in areas of more rugged climate.

Just because it is small doesn't mean that a miniature rose must be coddled. Unlike hybrid teas and other large bush roses, the miniatures should not be planted in a really rich soil. Soil should be well prepared but manure may be omitted. They make good root growth, and so should be spaced a foot apart. I am inclined to believe that the miniatures prefer to have their roots in fairly cool or shaded earth, for those I have planted beside flagstone steps and on a low rock wall have done well for many years.

Miniatures need some sun daily, but I am certain that they do not want full sun all day long. The only plants I have ever lost were those that did get sun all day. In a partly shaded setting and protected against prevailing winter winds by their location, plants have lasted for years. They require little annual pruning, and varieties to date seem not at all susceptible to disease or attractive to insects.

One more distinction the miniatures have: they are the only roses that can be grown as a house plant. While tree roses are wrapped in burlap or covered with two feet of soil in winter, a row of pots holding Tom Thumb, Oakington Ruby, Midget or Pixie could be covered with blossoms in a sunny window.

There's a trick to having miniatures flower as house plants. Some nurseries handle a few plants and sell them ready to bloom indoors. And some rose nurserymen recommend that miniatures, like polyanthas, be forced into winter bloom only in a greenhouse. But any gardener can purchase freshly dug bushes in November or December, and plant them in pots filled with a mixture of soil and peat moss enriched with a bit of fertilizer. Then they are stored in the coldframe and left there in the cold for a dormant period of about two months. They may be brought into the house in February, placed in a sunny window and watered regularly. In order to bloom, the plants should be in a temperature of not more than 65 degrees and a reasonably humid (not too dry) atmosphere.

Primarily for good outdoor bloom, but also as possibilities for the house, the following modern miniatures are listed:

Red	Red Imp—crimson
	Robin—medium red
	Scarlet Gem—bright scarlet

Pink	Bo-Peep—deep pink buds, pale flowers
	Opal Jewel—light rose pink
	Sweet Fairy—light pink, fragrant
	Tinker Bell—bright pink

| *White* | Cinderella |
| | Twinkles |

| *Yellow* | Baby Gold Star—may grow 2 feet tall |
| | Pixie Gold |

All except Baby Gold Star average eight inches in height, but under some conditions and in some years they may reach a foot.

Chapter V

Modern Groups

NEW VARIETIES of roses are commonplace, and it's a rare year during which at least a dozen new names aren't patented. But an entirely new race of roses, consisting of any number of named varieties that have distinctly different flowers opening on bushes with a distinctly different habit of growth from any others known heretofore, is so unusual an achievement that it should not be expected oftener than once a generation. Yet since 1935 two new races or groups or classes of roses have been developed by the hybridists, introduced by the nurserymen and accepted wholeheartedly by the public. These are the grandiflora and the floribunda roses.

Their introduction and development has not happened by chance. It has come about because hybridizers and nurserymen have keen eyes for plants that will perform well in the average garden and, above all, because hybridizers have listened to what the rose-growing public wants. The credit belongs to no one hybridizer or nurseryman. As a matter of fact, both American and European hybridists have contributed varieties to both the floribunda and grandiflora classes. Both groups, however, were christened and launched in this country.

Certainly no group of roses was ever more tailored to meet the demands of the public than the grandifloras. The class was born officially and the name determined at the 1953 annual meeting of the American Association of Nurserymen. It was presented to the public in 1954. Early that year Herbert C. Swim, California hybridist who had originated two of the varieties included in the new grandiflora class, wrote: "Since homemakers of today are finding more uses for roses [as cut flowers indoors as well as display outdoors] but often no more space to grow them, we need new varieties that produce more flowers of medium size, with longer-lasting qualities on more disease-resistant plants." That is quite an order, but Mr. Swim's own standards for a good rose include other endearing qualities, such as true fragrance and beautiful bud as well as flower form.

Not everyone may be as insistent on the two latter characteristics in a rose as Mr. Swim is, but his statement is a pretty good description of any grandiflora rose. The bushes are, above all, free-flowering and bloom continuously. In the East, for example, a grandiflora variety does not lack bloom from sometime in June until frost freezes the buds in late October or November.

The roses usually appear in clusters, but then again the same bush may have flowers in clusters and some stems with only one flower. The flowers are always double, with an average of 24 to 36 petals. This ranks them as medium in size or, to quote the standard, "not necessarily as large as a hybrid tea, but larger than the average floribunda, with hybrid tea standard for bud and flower form." Whether they bear one or several flowers, the stems are always long enough for cutting and for effective flower arrangements.

Grandiflora bushes grow relatively tall. Three to four feet is average, but in some climates and soils the canes may shoot up to six feet. Foliage is luxuriant and clean. Whether three or six feet tall, the stems are well clothed with leaves from bottom to top. Most important of all, this foliage is clean-looking at all times, and under normal conditions appears reasonably resistant to disease. In my own experience, in four years six bushes of Carrousel, the first grandiflora variety, have never been touched with black spot, the most devastating enemy of roses in my garden.

When a rose performs as Carrousel does for me, when I can see its crimson flowers every day for five months, it naturally belongs on a list of roses I wouldn't be without. Greater recognition was given to another variety in 1954, the year the grandiflora class was officially introduced to the public, for the pink Queen Elizabeth won an All-America Selections Award, the highest honor that can be bestowed in this country. The yellow variety Buccaneer earlier had won fame abroad, for it received the gold medal of the Concours Internationale des Roses Nouvelles de Genève.

Awards have been accruing to the floribundas ever since 1940, when the red variety World's Fair won the first All-America Selections Award for its then almost new rose class. This perhaps was a clinching argument, for the thirties had seen considerable bickering and discussion, particularly about the name and the class, floribunda.

Hybrid Tea Rose

Floribunda Rose

TYPES OF BUSHES AND HABITS OF GROWTH

Actually it is a most descriptive and appropriate name for this group. Floribunda, meaning "flowers in abundance," was chosen by the late Dr. J. H. Nicolas, then director of research for Jackson & Perkins, rose growers in Newark, N. Y. Dr. Nicolas was not only the hybridist who originated several of the early floribunda varieties, but he did perhaps more than anyone else to establish the class.

Dr. Nicolas selected the name to describe varieties which, for the most part, had been obtained by the crossing of the small and cluster-flowered polyantha roses with the large, one-blossom-on-each-stem hybrid teas. Floribundas always open their flowers in clusters but the blossoms may be single or double, according to variety.

Floribundas as well as grandifloras are noted for their continuous bloom, which is from June to November in the Northeast. The quality of fragrance varies as it does in any class of roses. Most of the floribunda varieties—or at least the taller-growing ones—are good for cutting too. One of the favorite bouquets in my own home is the two-toned pink floribunda Betty Prior combined with Queen Anne's lace.

Floribunda plants are, for the most part, vigorous and hardy. I believe, however, that some varieties introduced within the last few years are not nearly as hardy and vigorous as varieties introduced in the first ten years of the floribunda's climb to popularity. Some varieties, including Betty and Donald Prior, Summer Snow, World's Fair and Vogue, are far less susceptible to disease than others.

Their use as summer-flowering shrubs was a strong selling point in popularizing the floribundas, and their growth is indeed shrubby. They can be divided fairly well into two groups, according to the height to which they grow. One group is rather low-growing, reaching 18 to 30 inches. The other is much taller and cannot possibly be kept at a height of less than four feet. Betty Prior, Salmon Spray, Jiminy Cricket and Floradora grow from any one spring to the succeeding autumn as tall and as broad as a forsythia or bridal wreath. On the other hand, Goldilocks, Garnette, Summer Snow and China Doll provide a neat hem of bloom for a walk, driveway or bed of hybrid tea roses.

Almost forgotten in the greater beauty and effectiveness of the floribundas and grandifloras is the much older group known as polyanthas. The polyanthas are an acknowledged parent of the original floribundas and, therefore, probably some of their blood is to be found in the newer grandifloras. The polyanthas themselves are a cross primarily between Rosa multiflora from Japan and R. chinensis, a highly variable species from China. But since the first one was introduced

Climbing Rose Shrub Rose

TYPES OF BUSHES AND HABITS OF GROWTH

in 1875, they have been crossed with so many kinds of roses that modern polyanthas have exceedingly mixed blood.

The named varieties of polyanthas are not variable. And in spite of the overwhelming popularity of floribundas and grandifloras, most catalogues still list half a dozen varieties of polyanthas. It's a rare year, too, when polyanthas aren't seen at Eastertime, having been forced into early bloom and being sold as pot plants. For some reason, these forced plants usually are called "baby ramblers." They don't ramble, although they do grow vigorously. More often than not these Easter plants have strong orange-scarlet flowers. This tone is typical of the polyanthas, and is best known in the old variety

Gloria Mundi and in the newer, larger-flowered Orange Triumph.

Other colors are included in the polyantha range, as well as one of the most famous of all rose varieties. This is the delicate, light pink Cecile Brunner, which no one ever calls anything but the "sweetheart rose."

Whether it is exquisite Cecile Brunner or flaming Orange Triumph, polyantha roses always bloom in clusters and the blossoms are comparatively small. No polyantha blossom is ever more than two inches wide when fully open, and often it is no more than an inch. One of the smallest-flowered varieties, distinct for both its color and form, is Margo Koster. This has perfect globes of flowers, no more than an inch wide, and a delightful pink-orange tint.

All of the polyantha varieties bloom continuously too, and because the plants are low-growing and branch like shrubs, they are fine for a mass effect of color. Few, if any of the varieties now in commerce grow more than eighteen inches tall, or at best two feet. Plants are vigorous and hardy.

Cutting the flowers is the most regular attention needed by the floribundas and grandifloras, and that is really a pleasure, not a chore. Since polyantha bloom generally is left for display, this class sounds as though it is no work at all to maintain. It is true that this class, and also the grandifloras and floribundas, give the most bloom for the least work.

All varieties in each class need little pruning in spring— usually only enough to remove any dead wood and perhaps to make the bushes more shapely. They will need the annual periodic fertilizing, but little if any spraying or dusting. Diseases are not too likely, particularly with the grandifloras, and insects seldom really spoil the bloom. There are bound to be aphids on the buds sometime between May and October, but if there is no time free to spray these little sucking pests into oblivion, then sooner or later the ladybugs or sparrows will come along and feast on the aphids.

Another new class—hedge roses—is building up slowly. Certainly the few entries so far are better for the purpose than space-consuming Rosa multiflora. Satisfactory boundaries, both east and west, are provided by Red Glory, growing about five feet tall, and County Fair, about three feet. Bushes are fast-growing, compact and produce semi-double red and bright pink roses respectively throughout the flowering season.

The polyantha, floribunda and grandiflora races grow and flower well in all parts of the country. There is no need, therefore, to select varieties for different regions, according to whether they have cold winters, or hot or humid summers.

Grandiflora

Ten years have brought many varieties. Superior performance may be expected from:

Red

Carrousel—*crimson*
El Capitan—*fiery red*
Floriade—*orange scarlet*
John S. Armstrong—*dark red*
Roundelay—*cardinal red*
Starfire—*cherry red*
War Dance—*orange red*

Pink

Camelot—*coral pink*
Montezuma—*orange-salmon
    blend*
Pink Parfait—*shades of pink*
Queen Elizabeth—*soft pink*
Yellow—Buccaneer
                Golden Girl
White—Mt. Shasta

Floribunda

Of the innumerable varieties on the market, the following
are among the outstanding ones for performance and dura-
bility:

Tall—4 feet

Betty Prior—single; *light pink* above, *rose* beneath
Fire King—double; *orange red*
Jiminy Cricket—double; *salmon orange*
Little Darling—double; *yellow, rose-pink* blend
Spartan—double; *orange red*
Vogue—double; *cherry rose*

Low—18-30 inches

Circus—double; *multi-colored*
Goldilocks—double; *yellow*
Moonsprite—double; *pale gold* center, *white* at edge
Sarabande—semi-single; *orange red*
Saratoga—large double; *white*
Valentine—semi-double; *bright red*

Polyantha

Cecile Brunner—*light pink*
Margo Koster—*salmon orange*
Orange Triumph—*scarlet orange*
The Fairy—*shell pink*

Chapter VI

Old Roses

THE FIRST ROSEBUSHES anyone coming to visit me sees are two shrubs flanking the driveway. These are Rosa hugonis, a rose first sent from China to England in 1899. Behind these shrubs on one side of the driveway is a line of Carrousel, an American debutante of 1952, and on the other side a row of Redcap, an American of 1955. I chose R. hugonis, sometimes called Father Hugo's rose or the Golden Rose of China, because it blooms in May with the lilacs that are all around.

The Golden Rose of China is a lovely rose with an interesting history. But anyone who wanted to grow an interesting historical rose could choose any number that would be worthwhile. It might be a plant of R. gallica, which is said to be the first named rose, back in A. D. 1350, and was the one whose pink or red petals were used so lavishly by the Romans. Or it might be Kazanlik, a damask rose whose petals are gathered in the Balkans to make attar of roses for perfumes. Or it might be Old Blush, which is the one the poet Thomas Moore referred to as "the last rose of summer." Or it might be a moss rose, perhaps the crested moss called Chapeau de Napoleon, which Josephine cultivated in her famous rose garden at Malmaison. Or there's the eglantine or sweet brier (R. eglanteria), which scented the gardens of Elizabeth I of England and which probably shaded the bank of Shakespeare's Titania.

The mere fact that it has a fascinating history or is linked to one of the great persons of the ages or has ineffable fragrance isn't enough to make a rose worth growing today. But there are dozens of old species, strains and varieties that are beautiful, even by present-day standards, and useful.

As a group, the species (or native), the shrub and the old-fashioned roses are diverse in their habit of growth and even more diverse in their flowering. Among them is not only Father Hugo, with single five-petaled yellow flowers, but the hundred-petaled rosy pink cabbage rose (R. centifolia). The common name "cabbage" derives not from the size but from the round, incurved shape of the blooms. There is the York and Lancaster, on which any blossom may have petals entirely white, or entirely red, or blossoms both red and white. Easier to locate today is Rosa Mundi, its pink petals striped or blotched with red and rose.

Fragrance is a hallmark of these old roses. Smelling even the plainest-looking one can be a treat to present-day gardeners, who may have forgotten what true rose fragrance is in the flashy beauty of such hybrid teas as Chrysler Imperial or Centennial. Peers of the true, rich rose fragrance are the cabbage, moss and damask roses. The little Scotch rose (R. spinosissima) is fragrant beyond belief, and the eglantine or sweetbrier is noted even for the delicious scent of its young foliage.

Perhaps no other group of roses is so noted, either, for its fruits. Many of the shrub and species roses develop large hips, or seed pods, which turn an attractive red in early fall. The Rugosas, for example, are particularly handsome when hips are ripe.

Some people collect these old roses by hunting about farmhouses and old cemeteries, by exchanging slips with other collectors far and near, or simply by buying from a few nurseries that still specialize in them. The finest collection I have seen is part of the planting at Descanso Gardens at La Canada, California, which are open to the public. There Old Blush blooms practically all winter. Some of these old roses are part and parcel of our modern ones, for they have been used by the hybridists for centuries. And within the last few years, strangely enough, a few new varieties have been added to some of these old and supposedly outdated classes.

There are many new roses that I would not want to be without, but by the same token there are a few old roses that would be indispensable for any garden I might ever have anywhere. This isn't because of any historical significance, romantic notions or even beauty of flower. Some of these old roses are useful anywhere because of their adaptability for hedges or specimen shrubs or because of their thriftiness under various climatic conditions.

One of the best examples of adaptability to climate is the Rugosa roses. They grow exceptionally well along the East Coast and thrive so well on sand, salt and wind that they are one of the few shrubs recommended for seaside gardens. The

Rugosas also are good as hedges or thorny barriers farther inland. But even though the flowers of some varieties are lovely, their casual growth and tendency to sucker do not recommend them for planting in a rose garden or with other types of roses. They belong by themselves as a hedge.

The original Rosa rugosa from Asia had single, rosy mauve or rosy crimson flowers which opened wide to show golden stamens. Its foliage was rather coarse and wrinkled, as is that of all Rugosas, its stems lined with thorns. There is a single white (R. rugosa alba) and a semi-double white (R. rugosa alba plena). All are remontant in bloom and all are unusually fragrant.

Handsomer in bloom probably are certain hybrid varieties of Rugosa. Among them are Conrad Ferdinand Meyer, with large, double, silvery pink, fragrant roses, and Nova Zembla, a white sport. Agnes, with coppery yellow buds opening to amber blossoms, is lovely. Sir Thomas Lipton, white, and Sarah Van Fleet, rose pink, are also good.

Having Rugosa parentage, but very different flowerwise, are the Grootendorst roses. These bushes, similar in appearance and growth to the Rugosas, are covered in June with clusters of small, fringed flowers. F. J. Grootendorst is red, Pink Grootendorst is shell pink. Both are remontant, if not continuous in bloom.

Blooming earlier than the Rugosas and their hybrids are certain truly shrub roses. First to flower in the East is R. ecae, or R. primula. Its erect, leafy stems are covered with single pale yellow blossoms. Opening two to four weeks later is the deeper Golden Rose of China. Its arching branches are lined with single yellow flowers. About a week later comes the semi-double and even deeper Harison's Yellow. Bushes of Harison's Yellow are more straggling than those of the two earlier blooming yellows, but it flowers even more abundantly, and it is still to be found, at the advanced age of some 125 years or more, from the White Mountains to the Rocky Mountains.

The Golden Rose of China (R. hugonis) is perhaps a perfect example of a shrub rose. It reaches six to eight feet in height and arches over gracefully; the stems are slender and thorny, the foliage small and fine. It is both neat and shapely and, therefore, splendid as a specimen shrub near a door, gate or driveway. Or if room is allowed, it grows well with other shrubs in sun, and is as hardy and clean as forsythia.

There are other good shrub roses that are almost as shapely. One of the best is the Scotch rose (R. spinosissima), which makes a fine three- to four-foot bush or hedge. The small white flowers, sometimes tinged with pink or yellow, are followed by little black hips. Bloom is exceptionally sweet-scented. The white form Altaica has larger flowers on taller bushes (six feet). Some modern varieties of Scotch rose, developed in Europe, are beginning to reach this country. One, called Fruehling's Gold, with cupped golden flowers, is certainly a candidate for modern gardens wherever a shrub can be used.

Probably the eglantine or sweetbrier rose was one of the shrubs brought to this country by the first colonists. This is the one with fragrant foliage as well as fragrant white or pink roses. Although bushes are long-lived and graceful, the foliage is nowadays susceptible in this country to fungus diseases. Also needing to be sprayed is the handsome Austrian Copper. In June it is loaded with dazzling single flowers, with petals brilliant red on top and vivid yellow beneath. I have not found Austrian Copper very hardy in Connecticut, where perhaps it does not like the open winters, but it certainly thrives in Eastern Colorado.

Not quite as dazzling but also very striking in color is the modern shrub rose Oratam, originated by M. R. Jacobus in New Jersey. The orange coppery flowers have the sweet damask fragrance. The foliage is good-looking, thus providing a handsome shrub for specimen or hedge. I grow Oratam now in place of Austrian Copper; both roses bloom only in June.

Less refined than any of these shrub roses and less worthy of being used for a hedge is R. multiflora. This plant, however, has gained a certain fame in recent years as "the living fence." It does make an impenetrable barrier, but not the sort I would want or would recommend as a fence or hedge in the suburbs.

The Multiflora is a wild rose shrub from Japan and China. It is strong-growing and vigorous, with long branches that reach as high as eight feet and then may arch over toward the ground. It may grow two feet or more in a year. It also is likely within a very few years to reach eight feet in width. There are clusters of small pale pink flowers in June, followed by clusters of small, bright red hips in autumn. Multiflora is a formless shrub, never meant to be used as a specimen. Planted two to three feet apart, bushes soon form an impenetrable barrier.

R. multiflora was recommended by the United States Department of Agriculture to farmers for hedgerow planting. For this purpose and for bounding the spreading acres of field and pasture, Multiflora is excellent. It is vigorous-growing, hardy and clean, requires no attention, is attractive in blossom and fruit, provides cover for birds and small animals, and prevents soil erosion. Then in the forties an enterprising

Eastern nurseryman advertised R. multiflora as a living fence and the rush was on to plant it in the suburbs. A bush that grows approximately eight feet high and eight feet wide is decidedly out of scale on most suburban properties.

A far better choice than Multiflora for a hedge in a neatly plotted community would be floribunda Betty Prior or one of the hybrid Rugosas. Another good choice would be the four-foot shrub named The Fairy. This mound-shaped branching shrub is covered with clusters of shell-pink blossoms from June until frost.

Not as useful as the shrub kinds are the so-called old-fashioned roses—the moss, damask, Gallica, cabbage and China roses, whose species and varieties trace the popularity of the rose through the centuries. These are roses to look at and to pick, to smell and enjoy. They belong in a bed or border by themselves, not in competition with modern hybrid teas and grandifloras.

A few of the old-fashioned roses are still grown as a matter of course in the Southeast and Southwest where climate is mild. The China rose variety Hermosa and the Noisette Maréchal Niel are treasured examples. Maréchal Neil, with its fragrant golden yellow buds and flowers, is not hardy in the North. The everblooming Hermosa, with double, soft pink flowers, is hardier.

The other old-fashioned roses are hardy, but are little grown. All four major groups have innumerable varieties on record, testifying to their popularity in bygone days. A limited number of varieties still are available through mail-order catalogues of the few nurseries that specialize in old-fashioned roses.

Among the moss roses the choice might be the typical Mousseux Ancien, white Blanche Moreau or Crested Moss. Crested Moss or Chapeau de Napoleon has less fragrance than many other varieties but has an extremely mossy calyx. The moss roses get their name from the fringy green covering of the calyx and bud envelope. They probably are a sport of the hundred-petaled cabbage or Provence rose (R. centifolia). The species cabbage rose, not unobtainable today, has light pink flowers about the size of a small hybrid tea. Vierge de Clery is a white variety.

Noted for hardiness are the damask (R. damascena) and the French—or in the Southwest, Spanish—Rosa gallica. The famous damask variety Kazanlik is semi-double rosy pink. Mme. Hardy is white, sometimes flushed with pink. R. officinalis, double rose pink, is said to be the original Rose of Damascus brought back from the Holy Land by the Crusaders.

R. gallica, often used as a background shrub in the South-west, has large, single, dark pink flowers. These are the roses so often seen in paintings of the eighteenth century. The French or Spanish rose, of which there are many varieties, has a tendency to produce striped or mottled flowers, but never produces yellow ones. Rosa Mundi and Oeillet Parfait are typical of the striped varieties in combinations of white, pink and red. Duc de Guiche has flowers of light violet red or lilac pink, changing to a gray red.

A "blue" rose, incidentally, is sometimes advertised. This is Veilchenblau, not an old rose comparatively speaking, since, it was introduced in Germany in 1909, and—it is not blue. While some kinds of red flowers turn bluish or purple as they age, Veilchenblau always has clusters of magenta flowers that verge on a violet tone from the time they open. I remember that my grandmother had it in her garden as something of a curiosity, but she didn't tolerate it long.

Not as spectacular and not as likely to set the teeth on edge is the green rose (R. chinensis viridiflora). No one should rush out to find a bush expecting that it will produce flowers with the lovely texture of a hybrid tea but with petals tinted green, or even single blossoms of an off-green tone. The little flowers are double and are truly green, but their petals look as though they are made up of small green leaves bunched together. The petals, like the plant's foliage, have a serrated edge, but even though the edges of the petals may be tinted bronze, the flowers still are not conspicuous against the true leaves.

The old-fashioned as well as the shrub roses have a tendency to send up suckers. These do not produce flowers different from those of the plant, as do suckers from a hybrid tea, but only serve to increase the plant's girth. Pruning, therefore, in spring and perhaps lightly again in summer to curb growth is the main attention needed. These old roses are, for the most part, not only rugged in growth but also fairly untroubled by disease and insects (Austrian Copper and sweetbrier are the chief exceptions).

It is pleasant to use a true rose shrub here and there instead of the usual run of shrubs, and to come upon a quaint moss rose or a striped Rosa Mundi or a sweet pink Hermosa flowering among the sleek modern roses. And it is pleasant also to plant these shrub and old-fashioned roses, for no special soil preparation is necessary. Most of them flourish in not too rich a soil, so it is only necessary to dig a hole, refine the soil by removing stones and rough material, and water during the course of planting. The old authorities recommended that moss and cabbage roses be fertilized heavily, especially at flowering time, and the advice is probably as good today as it was in theirs. I like to give Father Hugo's rose a mulch of well-rotted manure about every third winter, but Rugosas and most of the shrub roses grow too vigorously to need much outside aid.

Among the thrifty and decorative old roses are the following:

Shrub Roses

Rosa rugosa, especially:

> R. rugosa alba—single *white*
> Agnes—copper buds, semi-double *amber* flowers
> Conrad Ferdinand Meyer—double *light pink*
> Frau Dagmar Hartopp—*silvery pink*
> Sarah Van Fleet—*rose pink*
> Sir Thomas Lipton—*white*

Rosa hugonis—single *yellow;* early-blooming

Harison's Yellow—semi-double, *gold;* early-blooming

Austrian Copper—bicolor, *red* above, *gold* below

Nevada—*creamy white*

Sparrieshoop—*pink;* bloom early summer to frost

Scotch rose (R. spinosissima)—

> Fruehling's Gold—single; *yellow*
> Fruehling's Morgen—single; *pink* and *cream*
> Stanwell Perpetual—double; *white;* all-summer bloom

Old Roses

Moss—

> Blanche Moreau—*white*
> Crested Moss—*pink*
> Nuits de Young—*purple maroon*
> Old Pink (Common)—*pink*
> Salet—*rose pink;* remontant

Cabbage—

> R. centifolia—double *rose pink*
> Petite de Hollande—small double *pink*
> Vierge de Cléry—*white*

French or Spanish—

> R. gallica—single, dark *pink*
> Président de Sèze—double *lilac rose*
> Rosa Mundi—semi-double *pink,* striped *red* or *rose*

Damask—

> R. damascena—double *rose pink*
> Kazanlik—double *rose pink*
> Marie Louise—double deep *pink*
> Mme. Hardy—double *white*

Chapter VII

Where to Grow Roses

WHETHER it's the quaint little crimped pink blossoms of a Dorothy Perkins rambler, the haunting loveliness of a big single Silver Moon, or the sleek and colorful beauty of a Helen Traubel or a Comtesse Vandal hybrid tea, there's something about a rose that delights the eyes and the emotions of the beholder. There are few persons who do not love a rose in some if not all of its forms. And there are few persons who do not plant a rosebush or two, once they have a house with some ground around it. In fact, some people who live in the same place for years never get over the habit of setting out one or two rosebushes every year.

Whether the property is to have only one rose or be planted entirely to roses, the choice of the site has a strong bearing on the necessary upkeep and the production of bloom. Given good drainage and soil, improved to the roses' liking at planting time, certain other factors make a location favorable. One is freedom of the area from roots of trees and vigorous growing hedges such as privet. Although some roses can surmount competition, a site that is threaded with roots of permanent plants such as trees is distinctly unfair.

Exposure to high winds, winter or summer, is another drawback. The choice of such an open site will be costly, for a certain percentage of bushes will be lost every spring because of winterkilling. Exposure to high winds in summer causes plants to dry out in such a way that only the sturdiest can survive, even if the ground is watered regularly. Steady winds shorten the life of the flowers too. In regions where wind blows almost constantly, it is best to locate a rose planting so that it is protected by a stand of trees, the wall of a building or some similar windbreak.

41

It stands to reason that roses, since they are flowering plants, need sun. The six hours a day—when the sun shines —requisite for a successful vegetable plot is, in general, an equally good rule for roses. The majority of roses will do about as well if they receive four instead of six hours of sun daily. This sun need not necessarily be full, bright sun. The sunlight that filters through the high arching branches of elm or locust trees, for example, is adequate. In fact, full exposure to hot summer sun is debilitating to miniature roses, I am sure, to some hybrid teas, particularly yellow varieties, and to a few climbers, including Mercedes Gallart and Aloha.

Public rose gardens are almost always level stretches of ground. This seems to be a uniform selection either for a rose garden in a public park, a municipal garden devoted solely to roses, or the display garden of a rose nursery. Such gardens, which are planted with hundreds and sometimes thousands of bushes, are formal ones. That is, they consist of beds—rectangular, circular, pie-shaped or some other geometric form— laid out with paths between them to form a pattern. The level height of bush roses is broken by the strategic placement of taller tree roses or climbers trained against pillars. The climbers sometimes extend along chains connecting the posts to make a festoon of flowers.

The formal rose garden is seen less often today on private properties. For those who like their orderliness, a small formal rose garden can be fitted into the smallest property. Consider the average suburban property 60 to 75 feet wide by 75 to 100 feet deep. At the rear or the side of the house four L-shaped beds, no more than six or eight feet long, might be set in the lawn and planted with hybrid tea, floribunda and grandiflora roses. A sundial centered among the beds serves as a focal point, the lawn as paths.

Whether the formal rose garden on a property is small or large, certain extraneous considerations help to give it distinction. Grass paths help to provide a setting, badly needed by hybrid tea roses whose growth may be rather thin. A low edging of evergreen germander (teucrium) provides difference in height and contrast in texture, conceals part of the thin-foliaged stems, and helps to tie the beds together into a unit. Dwarf boxwood in milder climates and dwarf yew (Taxus canadensis stricta) in colder ones are other evergreen possibilities for edging.

For accent plus distinction in the small formal garden, shrubs may be used sparingly. A pair or two of yew, for example, might mark the entrance to the main paths or serve as background if placed in corners. Tree roses or climbers against posts can achieve the same effect.

Formal gardens may be the traditional way to grow a large number of rosebushes, but this is frequently inconsistent with the present-day popularity of casual living and the use of the garden or the back yard as an outdoor living room for the whole family. And so the trend nowadays is to live with roses.

This means more casual planting of roses—all kinds of roses. It means not formal beds of roses centered around a sundial, but roses used purposefully wherever possible around the property. It means substituting the right kind of rose for forsythia or bridal wreath; it means setting out Little Compton Creeper instead of periwinkle (Vinca minor) to hold a bank; it means a few miniature roses in the rock garden in place of alpine plants. It means, in short, that on even the smallest property every class of rose can be represented.

Hybrid tea and climbing roses probably present the greatest problem when it comes to finding a place for them. Hybrid teas are the one kind of rose that doesn't thrive if combined with other kinds of plants. For hybrid teas do not like competition, and they need to be so grouped that there is circulation of air about the bushes in order to reduce the incidence of disease. This means that hybrid teas are best grown in a bed or a border by themselves. If the soil is right, it might be the strip between the driveway and property line. Or it might be a bed, two bushes wide, on either side of the front walk. It might be a border in front of the fence at the rear of the property (a green vine covering the fence improves the setting), or it might be a square or round bed, accommodating a dozen hybrid teas, as the focal point of the whole garden.

Climbers present a problem, for they must have some sort of support so that they can grow either up or down. Perhaps the fashion of rustic or white rail fences across the front of the property has gained favor just because such a fence is an ideal place to grow some of the lovely modern climbing roses, and especially the everblooming varieties.

Climbing roses can be tied and trained to trellises against a porch or on either side of a kitchen door. They can be fastened to a cedar post embedded in the ground wherever one would seem suitable and not out of place. And climbing roses as well as the creeping ones are not only good covers for rough ground but also good bank binders to prevent soil erosion. Climbers such as the single pink Mary Wallace or white Mermaid are charming if their canes are pegged down around the edge of a pool.

The other main groups of roses—floribunda, grandiflora and shrub—are adaptable and versatile, as far as placement goes. They are sturdy enough in their growth to perform well in combination with perennials and other shrubs, provided the roses are spaced adequately (page 56).

Shrub roses can be used anywhere in a sunny or partly sunny location where other flowering shrubs might be used. Many of them, such as Austrian Copper or the Golden Rose of China (R. hugonis), are both shapely and strong enough to be used as specimen plants. Others, such as the Rugosas, are excellent hedges or thorny barriers.

Floribundas and grandifloras have at least one advantage over the shrub roses. These two groups bloom continuously from late spring until late fall. They therefore are showy and can be used confidently in important places. The floribundas and grandifloras grow so vigorously that they can be used anywhere that a rose or other type of flowering shrub might be used.

Before deciding which floribunda to use, the height of the variety should be checked. Some floribundas, such as Summer Snow, grow only two feet or so tall, thus making them suitable for edging a walk or driveway or facing down a planting of taller shrubs. Other floribundas, such as Betty Prior and Salmon Spray, reach a minimum of four feet in height and thus make a better hedge or barrier planting, which might be as a group of three bushes at a corner to prevent cutting across a lawn. Grandifloras average four feet in height under average conditions.

Grandiflora and floribunda roses, because of their vigor and constant bloom, may even be used for the so-called foundation plantings, that is, the planting close to the house that serves to tie the building to the land. The low floribundas are especially appropriate for the modern one-story house which so often has a long low box extending across all or part of the front expanse. Both groups are perfect for either a high or low ribbon planting anywhere on the property.

Just because floribundas and grandifloras are so effective en masse does not mean that individual plants cannot be effective. One Fashion rose might accent a bird bath surrounded with green ferns. Or a bush of Vogue or Carrousel might be planted beside a gate or near a garden seat.

Some of the hybrid perpetuals such as Frau Karl Druschki and Mrs. R. G. Sharman-Crawford also are handsome enough to be used as specimen plants. And they, like the floribunda and grandiflora, make a satisfactory substitute for shrubs.

All three groups contain excellent hedge material. The hybrid perpetuals Frau Karl Druschki (white), Henry Nevard (crimson) and Paul Neyron (lilac-pink) would make a refined four-foot hedge. With them might be used either the red F. J. Grootendorst or Pink Grootendorst and coppery yellow Dr.

Eckener; or any of these three might be used alone. Many varieties of floribundas and all of the grandifloras will also form four- to five-foot hedges. For a taller hedge up to eight feet, Rugosa hybrids should be chosen. The selection might include pink Conrad Ferdinand Meyer, white Nova Zembla, snow-white Sir Thomas Lipton, rose-pink Sarah Van Fleet and amber Agnes.

Of course, floribundas, grandifloras and hybrid perpetuals can be used as bedding plants, just as the hybrid teas must be. In beds, all four groups can be used alone or in combination with the others. The polyantha roses are primarily adapted to bedding, for it is the mass of color rather than the individual blossom that is stunning. The one exception is polyantha Margo Koster, which grows only a foot tall, and so is well suited to edging beds of taller roses or shrubs, especially evergreen shrubs.

This wholesale use of roses, wherever a bush can be fitted in, is based on the probability of about six hours of sun a day. But while sun is preferred, the person whose property is shaded by spreading oaks or tall tulip trees need not despair of growing roses. There are some kinds and some varieties that will bloom in part shade.

The limitations extend not only to some roses but also to the plants causing shade. Trees such as elm, locust and maple that have surface roots are no neighbors for roses. Trees such as linden or sycamore, with a solid crown of branches and leaves, may need to have the lowest branches removed to permit light to penetrate to the flowering plants near by. Pruning and thinning of branches also facilitates circulation of air.

So much for the problem created by trees. It also must be understood that while certain kinds of roses will bloom in shade, these flowers will not be the sort that will win blue ribbons, even at the local flower show. But by way of encouragement, it can be stated that shade for part of the day does help to preserve the color of many roses.

The owner of a fine stand of trees who wants to grow hybrid tea roses can hope to have bloom if he purchases such red hybrid teas as Etoile de Hollande, Crimson Glory and Charles K. Douglas. As a matter of fact, the yellow or golden hybrid teas, Mrs. Pierre S. Du Pont, Mrs. Erskine Pembroke Thom and Ville de Paris, have handsomer bloom if located so that they get afternoon and evening shade. The old pink Ophelia and Mme. Butterfly have more perfect buds and bloom if the bushes are protected from hot sun by high branching trees through which the light filters.

Almost any climbing rose does all right when planted

against a building wall, a location where some shade is almost
inevitable for part of the day. But adaptable to part shade in
other locations are Dr. W. Van Fleet, Bloomfield Courage,
Breeze Hill and Aviateur Blériot.

The grandiflora, Buccaneer, and the floribundas, Betty Prior,
Mrs. R. M. Finch and Salmon Spray, flourish if planted so
they do not receive the midday sun. So do several of the shrub
roses, notably red F. J. Grootendorst and Pink Grootendorst.
Two of the native species are worth trying in shade. Rosa
blanda grows five feet tall and has lovely single pink blossoms
against glossy foliage. R. setigera, six to eight feet tall, may
be grown as either a climber or bush, and has single bright
pink flowers.

Whether his land is blessed with shade or sun, the person
who really likes roses will find the kinds that will bloom for
him. He may know the variety he wants to grow and have to
find a place to plant it, or he may have several spots that
could be occupied by roses and have to search the catalogues
for the right kind of rose for the place. Whichever comes first
—the rose or the location—a good match brings renewed
pleasure every year when flowering begins again.

Chapter VIII

When to Plant Roses

ROSES can be grown successfully anywhere in the United States. But that doesn't mean that all of us who have ordered roses for planting this year will actually plant them on the same day of the same month. Even if there were a countrywide rose day, it wouldn't be possible to observe it everywhere by planting a rosebush. Climate determines the best time to plant.

In all parts of the country every year a good many people will buy and plant the All-America rose of the year. In 1946 it was the hybrid tea Peace; in 1956, the floribunda Circus. There's only an outside chance that the same number of Peace or Circus were sold in Norwalk, Ohio, as in Norwalk, California, or Norwalk, Connecticut. Or in Portland, Oregon, as in Portland, Maine. Even if the same number of bushes were sold, gardeners in each town would plant them in different months of the year.

In Norwalk, Ohio, and Norwalk, Connecticut, any kind of rose might be planted in either spring or fall—if in spring, in March or April; if in fall, in November. In Norwalk, California, a rosebush will probably be planted in January or February, although it might be done as early as December or as late as April. In Portland, Maine, spring is the only safe time to plant, and mid-April would be the earliest at that. In Portland, Oregon, rosebushes are planted in November or in February or March. But it is likely to be after rather than before the first of the year.

It's all right to say that it is always safe to plant a rosebush in the spring—that is, if spring can be expected anytime after New Year's Day. For the planting of rosebushes begins in the Southeast in January and ends in May in the northernmost state. The best months for the various states, according to climate, are as follows:

December, January and February	—*The Southeast:* Alabama, Florida, Georgia, Louisiana, South Carolina and Texas
January and February	—*The Southwest:* Arizona, California, and southern New Mexico
February and March or November	—*The Northwest:* Oregon and Washington
April or October	—*The Rocky Mountain States:* Colorado, Idaho, Montana, Nevada, northern New Mexico, Utah and Wyoming
March and April or November	—*The Temperate States:* Arkansas, Connecticut, Delaware, Illinois, Indiana, Iowa, Kansas, Kentucky, Maryland, Massachusetts, Mississippi, Missouri, Nebraska, New Jersey, southern New York State, North Carolina, Ohio, Oklahoma, Pennsylvania, Rhode Island, Tennessee, Virginia and West Virginia.
April or May	—*The Northern States:* Maine, Massachusetts, Michigan, Minnesota, New Hampshire, northern New York State, North Dakota, South Dakota, Vermont and Wisconsin

Yes, spring is always a safe time to plant rosebushes. And the fact that most gardeners agree is proven by the numbers of roses sold between February and May each year. But in by far the most populous area of the country—the temperate states—gardeners have a choice of planting seasons, spring or fall.

In some few localities—Albuquerque, New Mexico, for example—either season has its hazards. And not all types (tree roses) or all varieties (white ones particularly) manage to take hold and thrive there. December to March appears to be the most favorable period in and near Albuquerque, and once a good variety is established it does bloom gloriously.

For years the rose experts have been recommending fall as a season for planting roses. They recommend it as being just as good, if not better, than spring. But sales indicate they haven't succeeded in making fall rival spring for planting.

The reasons in favor of fall planting are all sound. The first one is advantageous for all kinds of fall planting; that is, the soil is warm and mellow and, therefore, there need be no delay in planting when rosebushes arrive from the nursery. The second important reason is that fall-planted roses make root growth during the rest of that season and are established and ready to start top growth when warm spring weather begins. The third reason is that rosebushes are freshly dug in fall and "first come, first served" is always the motto to obtain desired varieties.

But good sense as all these reasons make, the fact remains that the majority of gardeners still wait and plant in the spring. Maybe the lack of enthusiasm is based on being just plain tired of the garden and ready to pop corn at the fireplace when November comes around, or maybe planting spring-flowering bulbs is enough for most gardeners to cope with in fall.

New Jersey nurseryman Robert E. Eisenbrown says: "Fall planting is somewhat ambiguous. To the nurseryman it means mid-November and even December, which many amateurs consider too late. Experienced gardeners, however, recognize that cold weather must be here to stay before roses can be set out safely. An extended period of warm weather might start the sap running and cause buds to break which, of course, would leave the bush wide open to winter injury."

Bushes are seldom, if ever, ready to be shipped to gardeners anywhere before mid-November. For no matter where the bushes are grown, it is late October or November before they can be dug. It may have been in California or Texas, Delaware or upper New York State, or somewhere in the Midwest that the garden rosebush was grown by a wholesale rose grower or nurseryman, but wherever it was, he cannot start to dig bushes until they are dormant.

A dormant rosebush is one that has completed its growth for the year and is inactive, or resting. Rosebushes indicate the approach of the dormant stage, which on an established garden plant lasts throughout the winter, by ceasing to bloom and then by dropping leaves. In temperate states autumn, with its lower temperatures and less brilliant sunshine than summer, brings on dormancy naturally. And so in wholesale rose nurseries in the temperate states digging the year's crop of bushes can start in early November or possibly in October.

In mild southern California digging does not begin until December. Even then it is often necessary to apply defoliant sprays to induce dormancy. One southern California nursery-man told me that his roses often are "sheeped"; that is, a flock of sheep is turned loose to eat the rose leaves (they won't eat them all day long, but will do a good job in a comparatively short time if allowed to graze on something else too).

In the important rose-growing area of Tyler, Texas, digging as well as shipping begins in October. And the rose growers in this area continue to ship through the month of April, with the peak busy season starting in March. But whether dormant roses are dug in October or December, and whether they are shipped in November or April, they go from the fields to the packing sheds to the cold storage plant. In cold storage rooms dormant bushes are stored according to variety, under carefully regulated temperature and moisture to maintain dormancy.

By far the greatest number of rosebushes are purchased as dormant plants, whether by mail from a rose specialist or at the local nursery or supermarket. Each year a certain percentage of started or growing plants in full leaf, and sometimes in bud or even bloom, are sold. In fact, this is the accepted way of buying roses at local nurseries in southern California, and also in Florida and certain other areas of the Southeast. In these places roses, like other shrubs, are bought by the can and are taken home in that same can of soil—it may be a quart or a gallon-size can.

In the temperate states pot-grown plants are available for a few weeks starting about May 1. These are rosebushes which the local nurseryman selected in March from his dormant stock and potted up in rich soil. Because for two or three months, he has fed, watered and taken care of them, bringing them into full leaf and probably to flower buds, pot-grown roses are more expensive than the dormant bushes so widely available in March and April. Pot-grown roses can be knocked out of their pots and transplanted into the ground successfully in late spring or summer, provided they are given plenty of water regularly.

It would be senseless to plant a dormant rosebush in May or July, even if one could be found. But pot-grown roses are a good investment if an accident or an emergency makes it necessary to replace a bush—or if June brings an irresistible urge to plant just one more rosebush.

Chapter IX

How to Plant Roses

A ROSEBUSH is no more difficult to purchase than a newspaper, an ice cream cone or a package of chewing gum. It makes no difference where a person lives—city, suburb or country.

Rosebushes may be purchased by mail from a nursery that specializes in this flower, or they may be bought no farther from home than the supermarket, florist shop or five-and-dime store. No matter where a person lives, if rosebushes are ordered by mail, nurserymen do their best to deliver at the most favorable time for planting. That's why rose-growing centers are packing and shipping from mid-December to mid-April every year.

The retail mail-order nurseryman in California may have customers in each of the forty-eight states—and so may the one in Pennsylvania or New Jersey. In any firm's shipping offices are tacked up schedules of planting times for different areas, as well as traveling times by parcel post, railway express and air freight. They also subscribe to long-range weather forecasts, the better to determine when customers in Idaho or New Mexico or Massachusetts will be able to plant the roses they want to plant this year. Wholesale nurseries take similar precautions to make certain that in the Gulf States supermarkets and local nurseries will have packaged roses to sell in January; in Ohio and New York by mid-March; and in New Hampshire by late April.

If a person plans to buy his rosebushes, like his groceries, on Main Street in his home town, he'd do well to prepare the soil where roses are to be planted, before he shops. In this the person who has ordered his roses by mail has an advantage, for he will have weeks or perhaps months to make ready a place for them. One thing is certain—rosebushes should go into the ground as soon as possible after they are home.

If the plants are bought locally, there may, of course, be a delay of a couple of hours, or even overnight. In that case, if the bushes are packaged, leave them unopened until the hole is dug and the soil prepared for them. If the bushes are bare root, bought at the local nursery, then fill a tub or pail with water and stand the bushes so that their roots are in the water.

If the bushes are received by parcel post or express from some distance, the package should be opened at once. Inside the outer wrapping, are the rosebushes. Until recently, the plants would have been packed together with moss or other material protecting the roots. Nowadays many nurseries wrap bushes separately or bundled in sheets of plastic polyethylene. In this case, the package should not be disturbed until the moment has come to plant the bushes. If they are in moss, then the strings should be cut and the packing and state of the roots investigated. Probably the roots are encased in sphagnum or peat moss or similar material held in place by heavy wrapping paper. Keep this material constantly moist by sprinkling with water, and leave the plants in the package and the package where it will not be exposed to sun, wind or excessive heat so that the roots dry out.

Roots are not seen except at planting time. But they are in one way the most important part of the plant, for they absorb the moisture and nutrients which enable the plant to grow and to produce flowers. If roots are allowed to dry out completely before being planted, there's little likelihood that the plant can ever start to grow.

Roses are not very fussy about soil. They'll grow in almost any kind, so long as they are fed. I've seen wild roses growing out of rock cliffs at the edge of a lake in New Hampshire and mirroring their single pink blossoms in the water. I've seen Rugosa roses covering dunes along the Atlantic Ocean with their bloom. And I've seen bushes of Austrian Copper in the alkaline soil of Colorado that were far bigger and far more luxuriantly covered with bloom than any Austrian Copper I've ever tried to grow in the richer and far more neutral soil of my Connecticut garden.

These, however, are only random examples of rosebushes that have made themselves at home and flourish in spite of adverse conditions. The roses that we plant in our gardens— hybrid teas, floribundas, grandifloras and climbers—are carefully bred aristocrats and deserve the best that we can give them. They are not inclined to be temperamental and are not lacking in vigor. Why shouldn't we give them a chance to

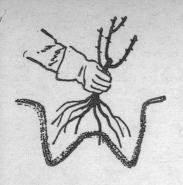

Make cone of soil in hole. Plant bush with roots spread on cone

Pack soil firmly between and around roots

Fill with soil to ground level and tramp firmly to pack soil thoroughly

HOW TO PLANT ROSES

look in our gardens as they are pictured in the catalogues?

The kind of soil is not so important, since roses will grow in soil that is either somewhat acid or somewhat alkaline. But a well-drained soil is important, and so is a rich soil. If it isn't well-drained and isn't fertile, both of these defects can be quite easily remedied. Most important of all, however, is the preparation of the soil. For the area as wide and as deep as the roots will grow, the soil should be loose and loamy and friable.

There's a simple test to determine whether or not drainage is adequate. This is merely digging a hole and filling it with six inches of water. If the water disappears reasonably fast, the drainage is all right. If the water stands, then the hole for one rose or the bed for several must be dug six inches deeper than is normally recommended. This allows for a six-inch layer of ashes, stones or other coarse material to be placed under the soil in which roses are to grow. To improve drainage in a rose garden of any size, laying a system of tiles may be necessary to prevent water from standing and thus suffocating the roots and eventually causing them to rot away.

To nourish an infertile soil is much less trouble than to improve a poorly drained one. All that is necessary is to provide plenty of plant food at regular intervals.

Whether it's for one rosebush—a climber perhaps by the kitchen door—or a row of rosebushes—it may be climbers along a fence or wall—a bed or roses or a whole garden of them, soil is prepared in the same way. That means digging —and digging to a depth of 18 to 24 inches. If it's rocky soil, like mine in Connecticut, a gardener is apt to stop gladly at 18 inches. If it's sandy soil, it's easy to go on to 24 inches.

If one rosebush is being planted, a shovel or a spade can be used to open a hole and place the soil at one side. All stones, tree roots or debris should be removed—not just from the hole but from the soil which will be put back in the hole around the roots later on. When the hole is deep enough, some well-rotted manure, compost, humus or similar organic matter and also some peat moss should be incorporated into the subsoil at the bottom. I usually put about a two-inch layer of well-rotted cow or horse manure (but only an inch if turkey or chicken manure) over the subsoil and spade this in. Then I add another two inches or so of peat moss and am careless enough about this so that some rests on the soil forming the sloping sides of the hole. The peat moss at the bottom is turned under and over with the manure and soil until the three have been incorporated into one even mixture. A handful of bonemeal or ground bone then is dropped in the bottom of the hole and scratched in lightly. Now all is ready for the bush to be held in place and planted.

It takes considerably longer to prepare a bed for perhaps six or more roses. Essentially the procedure is the same, but a spading fork is better than a shovel or spade to turn over the soil. Before any spading can be done, weeds must be pulled out, and stones and debris raked from the area that has been staked or otherwise marked out.

From this point on, there are probably as many methods of preparing a bed for roses as there are people growing them. I use a fairly simple method and it seems to give good results. When the top surface is reasonably clean, I scatter over it a light coating of a balanced commercial fertilizer (5-10-5) and an inch or so of peat moss. Then I start spading the soil, turning this top material under and over, stopping to pick out sizable stones and throw them away. The first time along the bed, the spade will probably loosen the soil to a depth of about six inches, but this is not enough. It's necessary to keep on spading, going a little bit deeper and working the better grade topsoil down under until all the soil has been loosened to a depth of 18 to 24 inches.

If simple spading does not seem adequate to loosen soil to that depth, then a century-old garden practice can be resorted to—trenching. Trenching is literally what it says. It means excavating a spade's depth for the width of the bed and putting the soil to one side (not on the bed). Then the soil adjoining is turned over with the spade and placed in the opened trench, and so on the length of the bed. When the last trench is opened, the soil lifted from the first one is carted around to fill it.

Once the soil has been turned over—by whatever method —it should be raked. And raked and raked again until it is fine. No matter how often it is raked, somehow there's always a stone or a bottle top that comes to the surface, and all such should be discarded. Once raking has been done to the planter's satisfaction, planting can begin. However, if a whole bed, big or small, has been prepared, it is just as well to postpone planting for two days to a week and thus allow time for the soil to settle. It is apt to drop an inch or so. Adding topsoil brings the surface up to ground level.

This business of settling, as well as of soil preparation, adds one advantage to ordering roses by mail. There's ample time, between sending off the order and the arrival of the plants, to prepare the bed. Those persons who believe in fall planting, but realize that they may not receive their plants until after the first frost, often prepare the bed during mellow October weather, and cover it with burlap or tarpaulin to prevent its freezing beyond the workable stage by the time the bushes are received in late November or December.

Having prepared a bed does not mean that the soil requires nothing more at the time of planting. As each hole is dug, I add well-rotted manure, peat moss and bonemeal, just as I do for each rosebush planted by itself.

Having given the roses a good start by preparing the soil thoroughly, it's important to space the plants so that they have room to grow. The experts' recommendations change a few inches every five years or so, at least for hybrid teas and floribundas. As to climbing roses, there can't be much argument about how much room they need. At present, the following spacing is generally recommended:

Hybrid Teas	18-24 inches apart
Hybrid Perpetuals	24-30 inches apart
Floribundas	18-24 inches apart
Grandifloras	18-24 inches apart
Shrub roses	3-4 feet on all sides
Climbers	6 feet apart

The place being ready and space between bushes determined, it only remains to get the rosebushes into the ground. The plants are taken out of their wrapping at this time. At no time are the roots exposed to drying sun or wind. I like to unwrap the bushes, drop them into a pail of water, and so transport them to their planting site.

Once there, each bush is examined for any broken stems or roots. If any are broken or damaged, they should be cut back behind this point with a pruning shears or sharp knife. This examination also shows whether or not a big enough hole has been dug. It should be deep enough and wide enough to accommodate the roots without crowding or curling them around. If the hole isn't big enough, back goes the bush into the bucket of water until the hole is enlarged.

There's only one way to plant a rosebush—and that's the right way. There can be differences of opinion about how to prepare the soil or about the best fertilizer, but not about how to go about the actual planting.

One person can plant a rosebush and do it just right all by himself. But it's much easier and much faster and much more efficient if two people work together on the actual planting.

One person holds the rosebush in place in the hole, keeping it straight and erect. The knob or swollen place above the roots but well below the point where stems start to branch should be just below the surface when the hole is filled with soil and the bed leveled again. While one person is holding the rose, the second person works fine soil in and around the roots, tamping it down firmly. This fine soil should be packed in tightly under the arch formed by the main roots so that no air pockets are left where water may collect.

After this, the person who put in the fine soil can fill the hole with water. When this has drained away, more soil is put back in the hole. When it is about half full, the soil should be stepped on to firm it down. Professional gardeners have been saying for years that the best rose planter is the one with the biggest feet.

bantam presents a portfolio in full color

SIXTEEN OF THE WORLD'S MOST BEAUTIFUL ROSES

Hybrid Tea: Charlotte Armstrong
Plant Pat. No. 455

Hybrid Tea:

Condesa de
Sastago

Hybrid Tea: Peace
Plant Pat. No. 591

Climber:
Blaze
Plant Pat.
No. 10

Hybrid Tea:
Simone
Plant Pat.
No. 1847

Hybrid Tea:
Chrysler Imperial

Plant Pat. No. 1167

Polyantha:
Cecile Brunner

Plant Pat. No. 851

Hybrid Tea:
Pink Radiance

Floribunda:
Jiminy Cricket
Plant Pat.
No. 1346

Floribunda: Goldilocks

Plant Pat. No. 1090

Floribunda: Pinocchio
Plant Pat. No. 484

Floribunda: Irene of Denmark
Plant Pat. No. 889

Hybrid Tea: Sutter's Gold
Plant Pat. No. 885

**Hybrid Tea:
Forty-Niner**
Plant Pat. No. 792

Climber: Dr. J. H. Nicolas
Plant Pat. No. 457

**Grandiflora:
Carrousel**
Plant. Pat. No. 1066

By this time there's no need to hold the rose in place, and the person who was doing that can either be examining the next bush to be planted for broken roots and canes or can be going to refill the watering can or pail. Meanwhile soil is added until the hole is filled to ground level, at which point it's time to firm it again, by walking around the bush.

Any raffia or cord holding the stems together should now be clipped. Whether or not these stems need pruning depends on the nursery from which the bushes came. Some nurseries prune top growth adequately before shipping the plants. If this hasn't been done, the gardener should do it. The general rule is to cut back stems to one foot if planting in autumn; to six inches, in the spring.

No matter which month of the year roses are planted, a cone of soil four to six inches high should be hilled up around the stems. This prevents the stems from being dried out by wind and sun until roots have started growth and have taken up their function of absorbing water from the soil to replace that which the plant loses to the air. The cone of soil is left around bushes planted in autumn as protection against winter. In any other season of the year, the cone is left for two weeks to a month. The soil should be pushed aside carefully as soon as leaf buds are noticeable.

It's amazing sometimes how soon leaves do come out. It's amazing, too, how soon bare-root roses bloom after they have been planted. From the third week in April to the third week in June—exactly two months—is all it takes in my southern Connecticut garden. And I am certain that in some parts of the country it takes even less for a Carrousel or a Sutter's Gold or a Tiffany to burst into triumphant bloom.

Chapter X

Annual Upkeep

N O PLANT so repays with luxuriant bloom the little attentions that are given it as does the rose. While it is true that roses bloom every year along railroad tracks and around abandoned farmhouses, the majority of modern roses respond best to some care now and again. Anyway, half the fun of owning roses is puttering around them.

There are chores—little and big, unimportant or indispensable—that can be done from the time the first leaves unfold in spring until the last ones drop in autumn. Most of these chores are seasonal rather than the sort that must be repeated over and over again. Pruning, for example, is done in early spring. On the other hand, none of us, no matter where we live, can ever get rid of spraying. And the bushes that need spraying most of all are the popular hybrid teas.

On the basis of spraying alone, it is easy to understand that some kinds of roses are more work than others, not only to keep healthy but also to keep growing vigorously and blooming up to standard. No class of roses requires more knowledgeable care in every phase of maintenance than the hybrid teas, for without such care, hybrid teas will surely languish.

At the other extreme are the true shrub roses such as the Golden Rose of China and the Scotch rose, which require little or no care at any time—no spraying, little if any pruning, and fertilizing only once a year. In this respect floribundas and grandifloras are halfway between hybrid teas and shrub roses. They'll probably bloom without any care at all, and need only a minimum to give a spectacular performance.

However many and whatever kind of roses are being grown, pruning and spraying are such precise operations that they are separate stories in themselves. The other chores are more routine, and are timed to the progress of growth and bloom. These chores are fertilizing, keeping the soil in which roses grow free of weeds, mulching, watering, disbudding and removal of faded blooms. Edging of the beds in which roses are growing is a nicety that helps show off their beauty to advantage. Edging, however, isn't essential in order to make the roses bloom, and that, after all, is why chores are done, though often with grumbling because it's a hot or humid day.

Weather, however, seldom makes fertilizing an uncomfortable task. This is one of the periodic chores that should be done three times annually for bush roses, once a year for climbers and shrub roses. Roses are fairly greedy plants and need this food to maintain both the quantity and quality of their flowers—no matter how inherent a characteristic is the vigor of the plant.

Hybrid teas need feeding three times a year. That isn't too much for floribundas and grandifloras, although they'll get along with two if time is at a premium. The first feeding should be given in earliest spring, immediately after pruning and at about the time the bushes are starting to leaf out. The second feeding is timed for early June, or whenever roses are really beginning to flower. And the third one is done in early July, as soon as the first big flowering has faded.

In timing of the last application lies one of two possible dangers from feeding. If put off from one busy weekend to another, it can be postponed so long that it would do more harm than good. This danger lies in the reason for fertilizing, which is simply stimulation of growth and, consequently, flowers. Growth doesn't start overnight, and so if fertilizing is postponed until late summer, young and tender new shoots could be killed by early frost. The last fertilizing of the year in the Northeast, therefore, is preferably given in early July and not, no matter what the alibi, any later than mid-July.

The second danger from feeding lies in the possibility of burning the foliage. It won't happen if the right kind of fertilizer is applied in the right way. If the foliage is burned accidentally, the bush will look sickly for a while, but it will recover.

Although roses are such a special flower, a perfectly ordinary fertilizer is entirely satisfactory. That is the balanced commercial fertilizer in the 5-10-5 formula (meaning 5 parts nitrogen, 10 parts phosphoric acid and 5 parts potash). Special rose foods, compounded of blood and bone and other nutrients that roses like in addition to the everyday phosphorus, nitrogen and potash, are available and are excellent. Anyone growing roses in or near Dallas, Texas, or in any of the Rocky

Mountain States, where soil is notoriously alkaline, will be wise to balance the diet by supplementary feedings of an acid fertilizer such as cottonseed meal.

Amounts are generally recommended on the package of fertilizer. Rule of thumb calls for a large trowelful or a generous handful of dry fertilizer sprinkled on the soil in a circle around the bush and far enough away so that none falls on stems or leaves. The fertilizer then may be cultivated lightly or else watered into the soil.

Liquid fertilizer could be applied to roses, but there is no particular advantage in it, and perhaps some disadvantages. Certainly it is less trouble to apply the dry fertilizer, and in the long run, it is less expensive than liquid fertilizer. In any case, I would give liquid fertilizer for only one of the three annual feedings—never in place of the spring one, but perhaps substituted for either of the two summer feedings.

Shrub and climbing roses do not need three feedings a year. One feeding is ample, and they'll flower magnificently for years if never fed at all. The chief reason for fertilizing either shrub or climbing roses is to maintain the quality of their bloom. A trowelful or a cupful of fertilizer sprinkled around each plant in spring before the leaves come out is adequate. Some years I mulch either the shrub or climbing roses, or both, in December with well-rotted manure. This always proves invigorating.

Fertilizing stimulates growth, and an adequate and even supply of moisture in the ground maintains even growth. In southern California and other areas where the annual rainfall is scant, and where the sun shines every day from May until November, irrigation is the common practice. Irrigation is controlled watering, than which nothing is more beneficial to plants.

In other areas of the country roses must survive all extremes of moisture—from cloudbursts and hurricanes to drought. Of course in southern Connecticut as well as in New Hampshire, New Jersey, North Carolina and many other states, there are years when rainfall is not only normal but is evenly distributed from spring through fall. But there also are years when spring or summer or fall is dry, occasionally so dry that it can be labeled officially a drought.

In Connecticut there was a drought in 1953. That was the year when, after an abnormally wet spring, rainfall stopped on June 5. We had a heavy rainfall (about four inches) on July 23, and not another drop until October 25. During that long dry spell, not one of the 200 or so rosebushes in my garden received any artificial watering or sprinkling. Yet Betty Prior floribundas bloomed all summer, as did other floribundas; the hybrid teas flowered intermittently, and then with their usual colorful burst in September. The flowers on the hybrid teas were smaller than usual by the end of summer, but they did appear. Nor did we seem to lose any more than the average number of bushes the following spring because of winterkilling.

I tell of this hot dry summer only to prove that roses are sturdy plants and can manage to live through even truly adverse conditions. I do not offer it as proof that roses do not need to be watered. If it had been possible to do so, I would certainly have watered the hybrid tea roses regularly between June 5 and October 25. But so often nowadays, when drought strikes or even threatens, a community forbids the use of water for lawns and ornamental plants. Such restrictions should be observed and, while they may mean the death of other kinds of plants, they aren't likely to kill roses.

The ideal situation would be freedom to soak the soil in which roses are growing once a week if it does not rain, and this I would do if I could. Once a week is often enough for it to rain—as far as roses are concerned—or to water. But watering should be the equivalent of a good rainfall, that is, enough to soak the soil two or three inches deep. A good soaking is fine; a light sprinkling, no matter how frequent, is no good at all. And the water should be applied to the soil for the roots, which can absorb it, not to the leaves and stems of the bush.

This means that sprinklers are not needed for rosebushes. The best source of water is a length of hose known as a soil soaker. This can be laid about the bushes and when water is turned on it seeps through the porous canvas hose into the soil. Not as fancy a method, but also practical, is to remove the nozzle from a hose and lay the end of the hose against a shingle or piece of tarpaulin to break the force of the water, which will then flow gently into the soil. After the soil soaker or hose has been in one place two or three hours, or long enough to soak the soil to a depth of two or three inches, it can be moved to another group of bushes for the next two or three hours.

As a precaution, even this sort of soil watering should be done in the morning, and discontinued after the noon hour. Black spot is far too prevalent and too dependent on dampness for its outbreak, to risk watering rosebushes at all in the afternoon or evening.

Watering encourages steady growth of rosebushes, and feeding stimulates growth and bloom. By the same token, watering and feeding also stimulate the growth of weeds. Big weeds and little weeds and grass—they start appearing in my rose beds in late April and, if unchecked, would take over the beds by August. Roses, not weeds, are what we want, and the weeds should be eliminated. This is, of course, primarily for the sake of the roses, but also for the sake of neatness.

There are two ways of battling the weeds: weekly cultivation of the soil or a mulch, or a combination of the two. Weekly cultivation means stirring the surface of the soil with a long-handled cultivator or hoe. A mulch is a two- to three-inch layer of clean material over the soil.

Cultivation of rose beds should be shallow, so that there is no possibility of roots being damaged. Weekly cultivation accomplishes three purposes: (1) it uproots weeds, leaving them to die in the sun; (2) it loosens and aerates the soil; and (3) it creates a dust mulch on the surface that helps to conserve the moisture in the soil. Of course, once in a while a weed will escape the cultivator until it reaches good size and must be pulled out by hand. But few weeds will reach any size if cultivating is done once every week.

By July, or even in June, cultivating can become a hot and arduous chore, and one likely to be shirked if conscience doesn't nag too hard. A mulch will accomplish the same ends as weekly cultivating, and needs to be done only once for the summer. I usually wait until sometime in June before mulching.

So the rose beds are cultivated in April and May, probably once every two or three weeks. Weeds don't grow as fast then as they do in summer, and rain is frequent (cultivating always should be done as soon as possible after a rain).

Then after a good rain sometime in June, the soil around roses is cultivated and the mulch is spread thickly and evenly over the clean damp soil. This mulch may be any one of a dozen or so materials. Peat moss is one of the most common ones. It should be soaked thoroughly before it is spread so that it won't draw up moisture from the soil.

In the Southeast the mulch is likely to be ground corncobs or bagasse. In lumbering areas it may be sawdust. Salt hay may be used, but is rather untidy-looking for summer. Buckwheat hulls are neat and satisfactory.

Peat moss is my preference, because I like its neat, clean, brown appearance. But after using it for two or three summers, I switch to one of the other mulching materials for a season or two so that there is no danger of the soil becoming too acid. (Considerable peat moss should be worked into the soil at planting time.)

Before the mulch is spread, and preferably earlier in the spring, edging should be done if it is going to be. Beds and borders do need to have their edges renewed or cut clean once every year if they are to look spruce and neat. Once a year is enough even if the bed or border adjoins a lawn, provided the grass at the edge is clipped correctly after each lawn mowing. An adjoining lawn or grass paths are the best reason for edging, for grass grows into the soil of the rose beds, making them smaller each year.

In order to edge a rose bed or border, a line, an edger or straight-edged spade and a rake are needed. The line is stretched between two stakes along the front of the bed or border where the edge should be. It's really essential to have a line, for the eye can not be trusted for cutting a straight edge. Then the edger or spade is pressed down to cut a straight edge along the line. Ragged hunks of grass or clods will come off and may be shoved over on the bed. When the straight edge has been cut the full length, the line can be taken up. Then soil is shaken from the clods, which are set aside for the compost heap, and the excess soil is distributed evenly over the bed. The edge itself is finished by pressing the back of the rake firmly against the fresh cut of soil.

Once the mulch is in place, it means that the roses can pretty much take care of themselves. Certainly they can from the first of July until December. For by July 1—or a few days later—the third feeding will have been given. No cultivating, no weeding—or at most an occasional weed which has pushed up through the mulch to pull out—and perhaps no watering because community regulations do not permit. That means there's nothing to do but spray—and cut roses.

Part of the pleasure of growing roses is cutting them to enjoy elsewhere than in the garden. Even if the flowers aren't cut to enjoy, dead ones should be snipped off the bushes as soon as the petals shrivel or fade. Dead roses on a bush are not good-looking, and the forming of seed discourages succeeding bloom and consumes some of the plant's vigor. The one exception to snipping off dead flowers are such shrub and climbing roses as develop large and colorful hips for fall display.

Cutting off dead flowers is one minor step toward more and better roses. To have the finest blooms on hybrid tea and hybrid perpetual bushes, there is also an important chore that precedes bloom. That is disbudding.

This is a simple chore and one that can be done while the evening stroll is taken about the garden. Disbudding means just that—removing buds. Each stem of bloom has one terminal bud, with two or four buds a little below the main one. These lower and smaller side buds should be pinched off before they reach any size, leaving only the large terminal bud to form a flower.

Disbudding is essential in hybrid teas if they are to have flowers that are comparable to the pictures in the catalogues. Many of the newer varieties of hybrid tea roses, such as Tiffany, Confidence and Eden, require far less disbudding than older ones such as Crimson Glory, Mrs. Charles Bell and Dickson's Red. But disbudding should not be omitted for varieties that need it and a sharp eye should be kept on all varieties. It is as necessary for remontant bloom as it is for the first flowering in May or June.

The floribundas, grandifloras, polyanthas and climbers do not require disbudding, for their flowers are supposed to appear in clusters. Hybrid teas and hybrid perpetuals, however, are supposed to have only one magnificent rose per stem. So disbudding is nothing to be afraid of.

There's no such thing as a bargain rose. And it's just as important to count the cost in terms of time and energy for upkeep as it is in terms of dollars and cents paid for the bushes. Care can not be ducked in any climate by anyone who takes pride in growing roses.

There are short cuts, yes, such as mulching. But the person who is too busy to do anything but cut roses for bouquets should never plant hybrid tea roses. Their care is exacting, demanding and never-ending. And climbers take a good deal of time for pruning and training.

Requiring least care of all—for pruning, spraying and general upkeep—are floribundas, grandifloras and shrub roses, and of course the miniatures. So the busy person should confine himself to these groups, or at least should choose from these groups for the bulk of his rose planting, and have only one small bed with a minimum number of hybrid tea roses.

Chapter XI

Possible Pests and Diseases

ALTHOUGH you and I may always have to do a certain amount of spraying in order to have perfect roses on healthy plants, there'll come a day when little or none will be necessary. I suppose there will always be the chance of "a worm in the bud, feed on her damask cheek" or an insect whose favorite food is a pink or a yellow rose; but diseases are slated to become a thing of the past.

Two groups of scientists are working to make the growing of fine roses less laborious and more successful. One group is the scientists who recently have been finding more effective chemicals to control diseases and insects. The other is the hybridists who include disease-resistance of plants as one of their most important aims.

The goal of hybridists may not be in sight quite yet, but that it is a possibility has been proved within recent years. Few of the varieties in the floribunda class, introduced in the late thirties, are as susceptible to disease as are the hybrid teas. And an equally great resistance to disease is shown by the even newer class of grandifloras. At least one floribunda, the red-flowered Chatter, even seemed to repel Japanese beetles when this scourge was at its height in Connecticut.

While we are waiting for this millenium of disease-resistant rosebushes, spraying is an essential chore throughout the growing season and in all parts of the country. Even today, however, the busy person or the dilatory one can greatly reduce the necessity for spraying by the kind of roses he plants.

Shrub roses, for example, rarely need to be sprayed for an insect or a disease from one year's end to another. Floribundas, grandifloras and modern varieties of climbers as a whole

Using a dust gun

rarely need to be sprayed for disease. Such spraying as they may require is occasional rather than regular—for aphids that may appear to suck juices from tender leaves in spring or beetles that chew the petals of flowers in summer.

It is the hybrid teas that require all the work. It is not that they are sickly plants, but it almost seems sometimes that they attract insects and diseases the way nectar lures bees.

In the East, throughout the Midwest and in the South—perhaps the prevailing humidity has much to do with it—black spot is the reigning disease. In the Northeast Japanese beetles are the most troublesome insect.

In the West, thrips are a downright nuisance. They are reduced, however, by the advent of hot weather. Then white fly becomes the pest and this, it has been said, comes with smog. The bad disease in the West is orange rust, especially in spring. Rust disease tends to defoliate plants, although seldom to the extent that black spot disease does in the East.

Almost anywhere mildew is likely to appear. This is the disease that coats leaves, buds and even stems with gray. It is particularly troublesome in the inland valleys of California starting in August, but in the East is more likely to appear toward the end of a long and humid summer.

East or West, no one chemical is a cure-all for the troubles that may beset roses. The same chemical will not subdue both chewing and sucking insects as well as diseases. Years ago, however, someone started to make it easier by packaging a three-purpose spray for roses. This consists of a good many chemicals, mixed in three bottles or cans. The contents of the first one are primarily for insects, of the second and third ones for diseases. Mixed in the proportions stated on the package and diluted with water, the three-purpose spray does a good job of keeping roses healthy, if applied regularly. It is available under several trade names, put on the market by different companies.

Spraying to keep rosebushes healthy starts as soon as leaves unfold. Insects are taken care of as they appear, but it is always easier to prevent a disease than it is to control it. To eradicate a disease, once it starts, is next to impossible. Therefore spraying should start early and be maintained throughout the growing season.

Spraying should be done once a week, or at the least every ten days, in order to control black spot and other diseases. If it rains within twenty-four hours after spraying, the job should be done all over again as soon as possible. Packages of spray materials usually say to use morning or evening, but the best time to spray, in my opinion, is in the morning. It may be entirely safe to dust in the evening, but I prefer not to spray, for this leaves the plants damp, a condition that can further the spread of black spot. Spraying in any season of the year at midday, when the sun is high, can cause burning.

It is possible to spray with a liquid or to dust with dry chemicals, and the basic materials are available to be applied in either dry or liquid form. Dusting is considered easier and quicker by many rose growers. Dusts, however, always leave a residue on the foliage, whereas not all sprays do. I am inclined to keep a loaded dust gun handy to use when time is short or in case of emergencies, but my preference is for spraying, for I consider this more effective.

Whether spraying or dusting is the choice, it is important to cover both the upper and the under sides of the leaves. After the chore is finished, the equipment should be cleaned thoroughly by rinsing with water. This will prevent the residue from eating holes in the spray tank and from getting mixed with different chemicals the next time around.

The equipment on hand for the ever-present chore of spraying or dusting should be the sort that seems easiest to use by the person who does it. Sprayers come in all sizes, shapes and materials. Their containers or tanks hold as little as a pint or as much as a gallon of water, with chemicals in proportion. There also are cartridges to be attached to the hose that are diluted safely by the force of the water from the hose.

There are small and large hand dusters, too. Also, a cardboard cylinder that emits chemicals on the dusting principle is available with ready-mixed, combination chemicals for all-purpose control.

New versions of both dusters and sprayers appear regularly. Operating on another principle is the aerosol bomb. One has been especially compounded for rose troubles, as has one for house plants and another for controlling night-flying insects that are so annoying on terraces of a summer evening. While aerosol bombs are quick and efficient, they are not the answer to spraying for anyone who has more than one or two rosebushes, for they are too expensive to use for a sizable planting. One precaution is essential: hold the aerosol bomb at least two feet away from the bush.

The choice of equipment to be used week in and week out should be governed not only by personal preference but also by the number of rosebushes to be sprayed. For example, I have about 200 rosebushes, of which a scant 100 are hybrid teas, and the hybrid teas need to be sprayed every week from May until late October. It takes me about a half-hour to spray all these hybrid teas, not counting the time to mix the spray. It takes closer to an hour to spray all the roses if an insect such as aphids is abroad.

The equipment consists of a water pail which holds the spray material, and a sprayer of the slide trombone type. This is the one that is attached to a five-foot length of hose with a weighted strainer at one end to hold it in the water pail and the two-foot-long sprayer at the other end of the hose. This setup is easy to carry around the garden. I also keep on hand a duster which can be used as fast as it can be picked up for an emergency.

We spray faithfully, week after week, with the three-purpose liquid spray. Sometimes in May and in September, a plain nicotine sulfate spray is needed for aphids. In June all the roses, including climbers, may have to be sprayed with a rotenone preparation to take care of little green worms. During summer, in addition to the three-purpose spray, we apply captan, which is the best material to date for combating black spot disease.

If I lived in California, I'd probably still spray every week. But it would be primarily lindane in spring against thrips and, in summer, a three-purpose spray, plus a special one containing sulfur and fermate for rust.

Fermate and captan are new names in the medicine roster for roses, and there will be newer ones in years to come.

There was a time when sulfur was the cure-all for all diseases. When fermate was introduced in the late forties, it was hailed as the best protectant against black spot. Now captan in liquid, not dust, form has proved far more effective for home gardeners as well as for commercial growers of roses.

No better control for aphids, the sucking insects, has ever been found than nicotine sulfate. For chewing insects, anyone anywhere can always fall back on the old remedy, lead arsenate, although it leaves a white residue on foliage. DDT is good against both sucking and chewing insects, although in time some kinds of insect seem to develop an immunity to it.

This build-up of immunity by insects has long been known. And so, because formulas differ slightly from one firm to another, it is wise to change brands of all-purpose sprays every couple of years. These formulas are changed, too, by the manufacturers to guard against immunity and to take advantage of new and more effective chemicals.

Chemicals, incidentally, should always be mixed in the proportions and applied in the manner recommended on the package. They should be tightly covered, labeled and kept on a shelf out of arm's reach when not in use.

Even with the greatest care it is possible occasionally to damage rosebushes by spraying or dusting. The factor behind such damage is usually the weather. Sulfur, for example, will burn if applied when temperatures are very high in summer. Almost any spray may burn if true drought conditions exist, or if it is applied not in morning or evening but when the sun is highest. The signs usually are burned or browned foliage. This does not last indefinitely, but while it does little or nothing can be done for it.

Fully as important as regular spraying, as far as disease is concerned, is sanitation. When bushes are defoliated by black spot, mildew or rust, the damaged leaves should be raked up and burned. They should not be added to the compost pile or left on the ground, for they are thick with spores of the disease and unless burned will perpetuate it. Dead wood that is pruned out in spring and any wood cut off at any time of year that has marks of canker or of disease also should be burned.

Not strictly a part of the sanitation program but certainly a satisfying procedure is hand-picking Japanese beetles. All summer long in my garden there is kept handy but hidden under a bush, a covered coffee can half filled with water, plus a few drops of oil to film the surface. Morning or evening, when the beetles are quiet, the can is carried around the rose beds and the beetles picked off every bud and dropped in the can to suffocate. No spray has ever been found to be 100 per cent effective in controlling Japanese beetles. If perfect flowers are to be cut, then beetles must be picked off daily. Spraying helps, but in addition lawn areas should be treated with a grubproofing chemical to kill the grubs before they emerge as beetles.

Japanese beetles have spread from the Northeastern States westward to Ohio, southwesterly to West Virginia and southward even into North Carolina. If these iridescent beetles ever appear in your garden, do not give up in despair. They go through a cycle, increasing in number for several years, but eventually their numbers fall off to a controllable population. I speak from experience, for I've lived and grown roses through the cycle's peak, first on Long Island and then in Connecticut.

Rose troubles in some gardens extend beyond diseases and insects. In winter, field mice may nibble on bark and so cause some canes to die, but this damage is not likely to occur if winter coverings are not put in place until the ground freezes. If placed earlier, mice are likely to build nests in such material as salt hay.

Some kind of mole, so I have read, is at home in every part of the country. If they are plentiful, moles are almost certain to tunnel under rose beds, and their tunneling is almost sure to break the roots of a few bushes and sooner or later cause their death. Mole traps are said to be most effective in getting rid of moles, but the best mole battler I have ever had was a cat. However, not all cats are addicted to catching moles.

Lists of possible insects and diseases, with their description and control, are given on succeeding pages. No one garden is ever going to play host to all of them. In fact, the majority will never appear at all in most gardens. Some years, because of weather, may prove more full of trouble than others.

It is best if prompt spraying follows identification of the troublemaker. (The State Experiment Station or the Extension Service of the United States Department of Agriculture has the most up-to-date information on the effectiveness of the ever-increasing new chemicals.) But even if spraying isn't regular enough to control black spot and the bushes are almost leafless by September, hybrid teas will continue to bloom. The bushes look awful, but the flowers are still lovely. Those who object to spraying or to unsightly bushes at the end of summer can always resort to planting classes of roses that don't need spraying.

INSECTS

Name	Description	Damage	Control
Aphids	Green, black or red. 1/16 inch long. Soft bodies.	Terminal leaves and buds curled and distorted. Sap sucked out.	Nicotine sulfate or lindane.
Japanese beetle	Metallic green with coppery wing. ½ inch long.	Eats holes in leaves, buds and flower petals.	DDT, Sevin, or hand-pick and put in can of oil.
Leafhopper	Wedge-shaped green insect found on undersides of leaves.	Leaves brown at edges, stippled white on upper side.	Nicotine sulfate or DDT.
Midges	Young maggots found in buds or stem. White.	Buds deformed, fail to develop.	DDT every 7-10 days.
Rose chafer	Yellow-brown beetle. Long neck. ½ inch long.	Eats holes in leaves and buds.	DDT, or hand-pick and put in can of oil.
Rose slug	Larva of rose sawfly. Small wormlike slug.	Eats holes in leaves and often skeletonizes them.	DDT.
Scale	Dirty white scales (soft insect covered with shield) on canes.	Sucks sap from climbers and some hybrid tea roses.	Cut out encrusted canes in spring. Volck oil spray with nicotine.
Spider mites	Tiny, red, almost invisible mites.	Leaves and buds pale, sometimes webby.	Rose dust or spray containing malathion, aramite or any miticide.
Stem borers	Gray-white grubs inside stem.	Shoots wilt and die. Borers tunnel inside stem.	Cut off wilted shoots below damaged portion.
Thrips	Small creamy brown insects found on flower petals.	Flowers speckled, buds distorted.	DDT, lindane or malathion.

DISEASES

Name	Description of Damage	Control
Anthracnose	Round, ¼-inch brownish-black spots on leaves or stems.	All-purpose rose dust or spray every week.
Black spot	Black spots, ½-inch in size, and fuzzy margins on leaves. Leaves turn yellow and drop off. Small black spots on stems.	All-purpose rose dust or spray every week. Captan or Phaltan. Burn fallen leaves.
Blossom blight	Gray mold on buds and flowers, often causing balling.	Cut off infected flowers. All-purpose spray.
Cane blight	Leaves wilt and burn brown along cane.	Prune out diseased canes.
Cankers	Brown shriveled areas in bark, sometimes girdled. End of stem dies. Starts at wound from spraying or injury.	Cut out cankered stems. Use sharp pruning shears.
Mildew	Grayish-white powdery substance on leaves and stems. Often on base of flower buds.	Dusting sulfur or wettable sulfur spray or Karathane.
Rust	Yellow green spots on upper leaf surface, orange powdery pustules underneath. Leaves fall. (Pacific Coast)	Dust with sulfur, or combine sulfur with fermate carbamate fungicide.

General program: Give dormant spray in spring, before growth starts, of 1 part lime-sulfur solution to 9 parts water. Then as soon as leaves unfold, start weekly spraying with three-purpose mixture to prevent, if possible, diseases prevalent to the area.

Chapter XII

Pruning

SOME PEOPLE find a pruning shears an irresistible tool. They can't bear to step outdoors with one without slashing away indiscriminately at any bush or shrub. Then there are those who won't touch a pruning shears if they can possibly avoid it. Since a pruning shears is one of the indispensable tools for growing fine roses, the sooner a person makes up his mind to learn how to use them properly, the better pleased he will be with his flowers.

All roses need pruning once a year. Some kinds of roses need more than others. In mild climates, almost all kinds of roses will grow so tall or so long that they need a good deal of pruning just to keep them within bounds. But whether it's in coldest Minnesota or northern Maine or in steamy Louisiana or on the sun-baked Plains States, all kinds of roses need a certain amount of pruning every year.

In temperate climate, this pruning is done is spring. According to any old saying, "Prune roses when forsythia blooms." And this is as good a rule as any. Certainly roses should be pruned before their leaves appear. In the Northeast and Middle Atlantic States pruning should be done in March and April. In my southern Connecticut garden, we've learned to do it about mid-April—not before—because high, cold winds cause considerable dieback if pruning is done in March. And we'd rather do all the pruning at one time.

In warmer areas pruning should be done sometime in winter. Pinned down more precisely, pruning should be done during the few weeks of least active growth.

A good hand pruning shears is the one necessary tool. I suggest wearing gloves and a long-sleeved shirt if a jacket or sweater isn't needed on the day pruning is done. A lopping shears is convenient and may be necessary for climbers and shrub roses, which have thick canes. Or a small sharp saw might be used instead of a lopping shears.

There are many makes of hand pruning shears on the market. Out of them all, sooner or later, a person is bound to find one that fits his hand best and seems most comfortable to work with. The important thing is that the shears are sharp and cut cleanly and are not rusty.

Equipment for pruning includes not only the tools but the knowledge of what to sever from the plant. "As the twig is bent, so the tree's inclined" can be proved quite literally by the pruning of roses.

No matter what class or variety is being tackled, stems should always be removed with clean, sharp cuts. (I usually make mine slantwise, not straight across the stem.) No ragged edges or torn bark should be left—these are signs of a dull tool or a careless worker. Stubs, a half-inch to an inch long, shouldn't be left either, for they will only shrivel up and become dark and unsightly. A lateral stem or branch should be cut off flush with the main stem. To shorten an erect tall cane, the cut should be made just above a leaf bud, again leaving not the slightest stub.

This matter of cutting just above a bud leads to one of the most interesting facts about pruning. Leaf buds appear alternately along a rose stem or cane. That is, one will be at one side of the stem, the next one above it on the other side, and so on. If the cut is made above a leaf bud on the inside of the stem, the new stem will grow toward the center of the bush. If the cut is made above an outside bud, the new stem will grow outward. This is important, for if all stems are cut above inward-facing buds, the center of the bush will soon become a tangle of growth. The majority of stems, particularly on hybrid tea bushes, should be cut above outside buds for more shapely plants and freedom for movement of air through the bush.

The first step in pruning is to remove any and all dead canes. If one is completely dead it is cut off clean at ground level. If only a part of the stem is brown or black and dead, it is cut back, at a bud point, to living wood. Additional pruning is for the sake of finer and larger roses. And for this the mode of pruning varies with the class of rose.

It is difficult to keep any rose from flowering. But if it's possible to make it flower more handsomely by a little judicious pruning, it seems foolish not to do that pruning. Above all, pruning is not a chore to be postponed. It needs to be done only once a year.

Hybrid Teas

There is no group of roses for which pruning is more important than the hybrid teas. Both pruning and disbudding are essential in order to have roses just like those in the catalogue pictures. However, complete faithfulness to disbudding does not influence the size and quality of roses as much as pruning does. After dead wood is removed, pruning can progress along one of three lines.

Light pruning means a lot of flowers, but none of them as fine as the plant could produce. Light pruning consists of removing dead stems or any dead portions of stems. All healthy stems are left, and they are cut back only to the extent of snipping off the twiggy tiptop of each cane.

Moderate pruning reduces the number of flowers in June, but each flower will be a little larger and handsomer than those that would follow light pruning. Moderate pruning leaves several canes, but in addition to removal of dead wood, any weak or spindling canes also are cut out at ground level. Then each remaining cane is cut back to a point that leaves only six or seven eyes or buds. This will probably take off about one-third of the length of each stem.

Hard pruning produces hybrid tea roses as glowing and handsome as those pictured in the catalogues. It means prize-winning blooms at flower shows, gorgeous roses to cut for the house, and the finest flowers the bush can produce. Hard pruning reduces the number of healthy canes to three or four. Then each one of these is cut back to three eyes or buds.

If you don't believe that severity in pruning can bring such different results in bloom, then I suggest that you try an experiment. Select three hybrid tea rosebushes in a row, preferably of the same variety, but if not, then three that are remembered as growing in much the same way. Prune the first bush lightly, the second one moderately and the third one hard. The resulting bloom will set the course for pruning in future years. Needless to say, I wouldn't consider pruning a hybrid tea rose any way but hard.

Pruning is a spring chore. But sometimes in summer a sucker cane may have to be snipped off from a hybrid tea bush. A sucker is a stem that appears suddenly and grows rapidly straight up through the bush. Quite often it grows, in no time at all, taller than the other canes, and its foliage may look a little different. If it blooms—and it may never do so—flowers will be smaller and different from the variety. Sucker canes should be cut off at ground level.

Again, although pruning should be done only in spring,

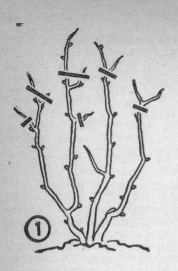

mild

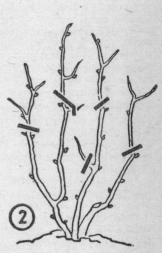

medium

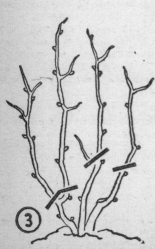

severe

PRUNING HYBRID TEAS

it is true that in some years light trimming is desirable in the fall. Weather conditions some years are so favorable to growth that canes of certain varieties of hybrid teas as well as those of hybrid perpetuals grow amazingly tall by the end of summer. If these stems are so tall that winter winds may cause them to tangle, and thus perhaps bruise other canes by their thorns, then the stems should be cut back a little. This autumn trimming should be just enough to prevent stems from whipping about, never more than one-third the length of each cane, and in no case taking the place of the annual spring pruning.

Tree Roses

Tree or standard roses should be pruned every spring as soon as they are taken out of their winter wrappings. It is the hybrid tea, floribunda, grandiflora or miniature that forms the round crown of bloom which is pruned each spring. It would be simple enough to say that one should prune a tree rose in the same manner as the bush rose of that variety is pruned. This, however, means little.

I have always found that tree roses flower most profusely if the crown is pruned hard. By this, I mean cutting back each stem to an eye or bud that is only the third or fourth one. This sometimes means removing half of the necessarily short stem in the crown.

Hand in hand with pruning goes shaping of the crown. All stems should be cut back to about the same length so that there is a neat round crown to start the year's growth.

Naturally the trunk is not pruned. But occasionally a sucker will shoot up from the base, or a leaf may sprout from the otherwise smooth bark of the trunk. Such leaves should be rubbed or pinched off with the fingers, and suckers should be cut off at the ground with the pruning shears.

Hybrid Perpetuals

Hybrid perpetual roses are, for the most part, more vigorous, more upright and taller-growing than hybrid tea varieties. Look at a Frau Karl Druschki (hybrid perpetual) and then at a Crimson Glory (hybrid tea). All the canes of Frau Karl Druschki grow straight up toward the sky—four, five, and even six feet tall. The canes of Crimson Glory are more spreading and branching, and the over-all height of the bush is seldom more than three feet.

All hybrid perpetual varieties grow like Frau Karl Druschki and all of them are vigorous. It's an axiom of rose pruning that weak-growing plants should be cut back severely, strong-growing ones lightly to avoid over-stimulation. Therefore, all hybrid perpetual bushes are pruned lightly.

In spring all stems of a hybrid perpetual may be cut back safely to two feet. This is true whether the canes are four, six or eight feet tall. The cuts, of course, should be made just above a bud, preferably one pointing outward.

Prior to reducing the height of the canes, all dead canes should be cut off at ground level. I also like to reduce the total number to four or five, cutting off those that are thinnest.

Hybrid perpetual bushes, in regions where winters are cold, snowy and windy, are much more likely than hybrid teas to need some reduction in height in November, for their canes can whip around badly in a winter gale.

Floribundas and Grandifloras

Floribundas and grandifloras require less pruning than any other class of rose except the miniature. And those little ones need only to have dead, twiggy ends snipped off, which takes only a minute every spring.

Because floribundas and grandifloras are so hardy, there are normally few if any winterkilled stems to be removed from them. That can save a good deal of time in comparison to the amount spent on hybrid teas in some climates.

Neither light nor severe pruning can affect the mature height of either a floribunda or grandiflora bush. The floribundas that grow four to six feet tall each year will do so even if they are cut almost to the ground in spring, and the varieties that grow two feet tall and stop there will do just that, regardless of pruning. Grandifloras are relatively tall plants, with canes averaging four to six feet tall, and they are fairly upright.

Pruning of both floribunda and grandiflora varieties then settles down to whatever trimming is desirable for shapeliness of the bush. Individual canes may also be reduced to any desired height. I like to prune such tall floribundas as Betty Prior back to a bud on a main stem, thus removing any twiggy branching at the tip.

Polyantha roses are branching and spreading. They also need only to have dead wood removed and light pruning for desired height and shapeliness.

Climbing Roses

Climbing roses of all kinds—large-flowered, ramblers and creepers—can be allowed just to grow, if there's room for them to do so. Pruning is essential, however, for both quantity and quality of bloom. It should be an annual pruning, as for hybrid teas and hybrid perpetuals, for it's easier to do climbers every year. After two years or three years any of them can be a thorny, tangled jungle to attack.

Pruning differs for each of the three main groups of climbers, both in timing and the material to be removed. The small-flowered ramblers need the greatest amount of pruning. Each summer they should be pruned as soon as possible after bloom fades. The pruning consists of cutting off at ground level every cane that flowered. If it's too hot in July or August to do this, it can be postponed to autumn or winter. The big advantage to pruning ramblers in summer is that it's obvious then which canes flowered and should be cut out. After pruning, the new and shorter canes are trained and tied to their support. Their growth continues through summer and fall.

Large-flowered climbers such as Dream Girl, Blaze, Doubloons or Parade need less pruning than the ramblers. The basic difference lies in the fact that ramblers bloom on new wood or new growth, and the large-flowered climbers bloom on old canes.

After the large-flowered climbers have completed their first big display of bloom, the side shoots or laterals may be cut off. That's all that need be done unless the canes are growing so long that they are reaching places where you don't want them to be. In that case, extra-long canes may be cut back, by as much as one-third of their length. Then canes are tied to their support, ready to display their summer and autumn flowers.

All kinds of climbing roses will need little or no pruning the first three years after they have been planted. That's because it takes any climber two years to show what it can do. After a large-flowered climber is five or six years old, it may need more than the minimum amount of pruning, if not every year, then every two years.

This extra pruning of large-flowered climbers consists of removing at ground level two or three of the oldest of the several main canes. These older ones can be told by their size, perhaps an inch in diameter, by the color of the bark, which is dark green or brown, and by their general toughness. Removing two or three of the old ones gives the slimmer, younger ones a chance to develop.

After pruning, the canes are trained and tied to their support—in the way in which they should grow. Soft green cord or raffia is satisfactory for tying. Twist-ems are also easy and convenient to use.

Creeping or trailing roses, as might be expected, need the least pruning of any kind of climber. They just naturally like to spread, and generally that's what is wanted of them. So there's no point in trimming back to keep within bounds. Every two or three years, however, it might be sensible to cut out some of the old canes.

Pruning of climbing roses, then, begins any time after June bloom. It certainly should be completed by the time pruning of hybrid teas must begin the following spring. The only attention a large-flowered climber or rambler should need in spring is tying to its support and minimum reduction of any canes that have made exceptional growth since pruning, or are out of bounds.

Shrub Roses

Shrub roses need even less pruning than the floribundas and grandifloras, if such a thing is possible. Shrub roses include the Rugosas and their hybrid named varieties, Scotch roses, Golden Rose of China, sweetbrier, Harison's Yellow and any of the old rose species or varieties that grow as a shrub.

If a shrub rose begins taking up too much space, as a Rugosa may, then cut off canes at ground level until the desired width is achieved. This can be done in spring or almost any time of the year.

Although almost all of the shrub roses are rated as hardy, nevertheless it is best to look over each one whenever the bulk of the spring pruning is done. This inspection dicloses any canes that may have been winterkilled, and these should, of course, be taken out at once. After that, stand off a few feet and look critically at the outline of the rose shrub. Here and there perhaps a cane should be shortened or cut off at ground level to improve the symmetry of the bush.

Like a forsythia, lilac or any other flowering shrub, a rose shrub will in time need rejuvenating. That means removing a few of the oldest stems to permit full development of the younger ones, and consequently more and finer bloom. Old stems can be recognized by their thickness and the darker hue of their bark, just as can the oldest canes of large-flowered climbers. All of these old canes can be cut off at ground level, or about half of them one year and the other half the next year when the younger ones have had opportunity to grow. This means the gradual renewal of the shrub.

Old-Fashioned Roses

Many people think a moss rose is prettier than any rambler of today. Often a cabbage or a damask rose smells sweeter than any modern hybrid tea. The experts of olden days had their rules for pruning to obtain the finest flowers they had ever seen. Two, three or four hundred years ago, the experts probably used a knife to prune. The directions given below for pruning the different groups of old-fashioned roses have been taken from the booklet "Old-fashioned Roses," published by Bobbink & Atkins, rose specialists in New Jersey.

Moss roses (R. centifolia muscosa) are said to have been given "most careful attention in the old days" and should not be neglected nowadays. They flower best if pruned hard; that is, cut back the canes to four or five eyes in spring before they leaf out.

The fragrant rosy pink cabbage rose, when seen in gardens today, is usually a shaggy and ragged-looking bush. But again, experts of the time when cabbage roses were popular recommended close or hard pruning.

Roses of the damask group, which includes the highly perfumed Kazanlik and the parti-colored York and Lancaster, make robust growth. They can be pruned severely, like the moss and cabbage roses, or moderately. Moderate pruning for a damask rose would correspond to pruning of hybrid perpetuals rather than to hard pruning of hybrid teas.

The French or Spanish rose (R. gallica) blooms on plants that are usually taller and more upright than those of the cabbage rose. But like the cabbage rose, R. gallica also should be pruned back to four or five eyes to obtain the finest flowers. It is also recommended that plants be thinned out at spring pruning time—in other words, some of the thinner and weaker stems cut off at ground level.

Special attention to the pruning of these old-fashioned roses is a small price to pay for these ineffably fragrant and quaintly charming flowers. In fact, the time spent on pruning any kind of rose is more than repaid by the improved bloom.

Again, however, the busy person who believes he hasn't the time to spend on pruning, or the timid person who is afraid of the pruning shears, should choose roses for planting according to this yardstick: The person who hasn't the time or won't prune shouldn't try to grow hybrid teas or ramblers. Hybrid perpetuals and large-flowered climbers will eventually prove disappointing if they aren't pruned.

With limited time for pruning, the most satisfactory roses will be the floribundas, the grandifloras and the polyanthas. And, of course, the miniatures.

Chapter XIII

Winter Protection

S IX MONTHS of bloom, five months without, and one month
when weather decides whether buds will freeze or open—
that is the score for the majority of people who grow roses.
November is the questionable month over much of the country. One year I cut a full-size Radiance the day after Thanks-
giving. The next year snow and cold froze colorful buds on
November 3. That day vivid Fashion roses, fully out, looked
silly encrusted with snow.

From December through April, roses flowering in dooryards are a possibility only in the southernmost states. Over
the rest of the country bushes are dormant—leafless as well as
flowerless. This period of resting, essential to the long life of
the bush, is known as dormancy. The plants are not dead.

Roses are hardy plants throughout the country, that is,
both roots and canes are capable of living through the winter,
whatever the weather. Classes and varieties vary in their degree of hardiness, however, and so a certain amount of winter
protection is needed in all except the most southerly and
equable climate.

Protection is needed, not so much against winter's low temperatures as against the alternate cold and mild, the freezing
and thawing weather. Of course, across the northern tier
of states and in Canada, low temperatures for a long period dictate bundling up, but through lower New England,
the Middle Atlantic States and much of the Midwest, winter
protection is insulation against greatly fluctuating temperatures. Could we be assured of a constant blanket of snow
from December 1 to March 15, not half as much covering
would be necessary for roses. The open, or mild, winters of
recent years in the East, when there has been little snow, may

have been a joy to commuters who have to catch a train five mornings a week, but they have been a hazard to rosebushes.

Wind can cause as much winterkilling as temperature. This holds true not only where winters are severe, but also in some areas of the Southwest where it is mild enough not to bother with covering if it were not for the steady wind.

Snow and cold such as came to southern Connecticut on November 3, 1951, merely froze flower buds and damaged leaves. They did not kill rosebushes. It is not the early autumn frost or late autumn blizzard against which roses need protection, but the extremes of the real winter months. It has always seemed to me that more bushes were winterkilled in March than in December or January. Sometimes a whole bush may be winterkilled, sometimes only one cane, and then again only three or four inches of several canes. If an entire bush is winterkilled in spite of having been given some sort of covering, the chances are it is not a sufficiently hardy variety for the area in which it is growing.

Hardiest of the family, even in the coldest areas of this country, are the shrub roses and the old-fashioned kinds—cabbage, damask, moss. Almost equally hardy are floribunda, grandiflora and polyantha roses. I consider miniature roses hardy and never bother to give them any protection, but that is because they are growing in a rock wall and in crevices of steps. I have had them winterkill when planted to edge a sunny bed in the open.

Climbing roses differ greatly in their hardiness. Ramblers and creepers belong at the top of the list with shrub roses. The great majority of the large-flowered climbers are hardy. Climbing hybrid teas are only semi-hardy. And of course there are many varieties of climbers—Cherokee, High Noon, Maréchal Niel—that shouldn't be planted even as far north as the Mason-Dixon line.

One of the reasons for the continued popularity of the white hybrid perpetual, Frau Karl Druschki, is the fact that it is so much hardier than the majority of white hybrid tea varieties in areas where winters may be severe. The hybrid perpetuals all are considered slightly less likely to winterkill than any of the hybrid teas.

The hybrid teas, however vigorously they grow and however luxuriantly they bloom the rest of the year, require winter protection except in the South. Above all, tree roses, whether their bloom is hybrid tea or another type, must have protection. The hybrid tea bushes must be sheltered against alternating spells of freezing and thawing, against wind, and against severe cold. In some parts of the country they need more covering, of course, than in others.

The amount of covering advisable can vary considerably within any one region, such as the Middle Atlantic States, and even in any one state, such as Pennsylvania or North Carolina. Less covering is necessary if the rose planting is on a property that borders Long Island Sound than would be needed on one in the Berkshires. And more covering is needed for roses growing in the high altitudes of western North Carolina than in a garden in Wilmington, North Carolina, which is along the coast.

Not only proximity to water, which tempers freezing weather, but location in relation to prevailing winds and the direction of prevailing winds are factors influencing the amount of winter covering necessary. To a certain extent, so is the kind of soil in which roses are planted. A light sandy soil, for example, is colder than a dark loam or a humus soil.

Here in southern Connecticut, five miles inland from Long Island Sound and almost surrounded by woods, I take care of winter protection sometime in December. The soil is a good brown loam, full of rocks—"for drainage," we always say. Every hybrid tea has a cone of soil about six inches high hilled up around it. So do many of the floribundas and the hybrid perpetuals, simply because they are interplanted with the hybrid teas. I will not grow a climbing rose that needs more protection for winter than a mulch of well-rotted manure over its roots.

There is no point in putting winter coverings, even the little hill of soil, in place too early. That keeps plants unhealthily warm and encourages field mice to make themselves at home. And if mice do just that, they may start nibbling at the bark of the canes before spring comes. Coverings placed too early encourage unseasonal growth, which will be tender and easily killed by real cold. The best general rule seems to be to wait until the ground is frozen. After this, the earlier in December this chore is done, the more comfortable it will be for the gardener.

Good soil should be used for hilling up around each hybrid tea bush. Since closer planting is now being advocated, it's a little difficult to take enough soil from between the bushes to do this, and, anyway, this has always seemed impractical to me. I'd rather push over to the roses a couple wheelbarrow loads of soil dug up from the cutting garden or wherever it may be possible to get some soil easily. At pruning time the following spring, the soil can be scraped carefully away from the canes, as much as is needed to rake over the rose bed to level it, and the excess returned to its source.

When hybrid teas and hybrid perpetuals are being hilled up, any extra-long canes should be trimmed back (page 77) to

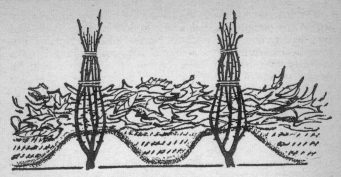

Winter protection in severe climates

prevent tangling and bruising during winter storms. Climbers and creepers, too, should be looked over for any extra-long, untrained stems that might better be cut back a little.

The question of covering, in addition to the cone of soil, is answered by the exposure of the garden and the severity of the average winter. If there isn't any soil available, then some other material will have to be used. The same materials as are used for extra covering may also be used as substitutes for soil.

Such materials for winter covering should be clean and capable of absorbing moisture, but not of matting as a result of it. These conditions eliminate leaves of any sort and manure for hilling up (not for mulching). Peat moss and salt hay are safe and sound. So are evergreen boughs. And evergreen branches are popular as covering in addition to the cone of soil, because they are light and permit circulation of air, yet are insulating. Pine needles and sawdust are other possibilities, alone or mixed with peat moss.

The cone of soil protects the heart of the plant from damage by wind as well by temperature. But if a certain group or planting of roses is exposed to prevailing winds, or if the location is such that there will be exposure not only to wind but also to the brilliant sun of late winter that may start leafing out too early, then a windbreak may be necessary.

A barrier to break the force of the wind in problem areas should be a planting of shrubs or trees. However, a temporary barrier can be erected annually and is not too much trouble if the planting is small. Sometimes evergreen branches stuck upright into the ground and frozen into place are sufficient to take the hazard out of exposure to wind and blinding sun. Other temporary and adequate windbreaks are a length of snow fencing or a screen of burlap tacked to laths.

No windbreak is sufficient to prevent tree roses from dying in any area that has a winter season. These are truly delicate and require real protection. Some people cover the crown with burlap or tarpaulin, tying it tightly in place below the point of union with the trunk. But safest of all, in my opinion, is digging up tree roses and burying them. This isn't too difficult, for roots are seldom far-reaching, but it does take time.

A trench six to eight feet long and about a foot deep is dug for the tree roses. This is lined with salt hay, the roses laid end to end in it and covered with more salt hay, plus three or four inches of soil. At pruning time in spring, the tree roses can be dug up with little difficulty and replanted.

Of course if anyone insists on growing climbing hybrid teas or admittedly tender varieties of climbers in approximately sub-zero regions, these also will need to be wrapped up. Choosing these roses under such conditions hardly seems sensible when there are handsome and hardy climbers to be had for even the coldest spots. But if tender climbers are being grown where they shouldn't be, the procedure consists of hilling up the base of the climber with soil, plus protecting the long canes. These long canes can be untied from their support and laid flat on the ground. They can be pegged down with clothespins or wire and then covered lightly with soil or with salt hay. Or the long canes can be left in place and cornstalks or burlap or even salt hay be tied around and against them.

Winter covering ends the chores in the rose garden every December. What, then, does the person who really gardens because he likes roses do until late March? Well, for one thing, he might have some pots of miniature roses blooming on a sunny window sill in the house (page 25). For another —and this he is certain to do—when the new rose catalogues start arriving in January, he'll be riffling the pages on dreary Sundays and trying to resist temptation when it comes to ordering more and more rosebushes.

Chapter XIV

Cutting and Keeping Roses

THE GREATEST REWARD for pruning, spraying and generally taking care of rosebushes—as far as I am concerned—is to walk out into the garden and cut one lovely, half-open rose. Close at hand in a vase in the house, its full beauty of color, form and fragrance can really be appreciated.

From the day in May when we can first cut sprays of the Golden Rose of China to anchor in a pin holder in a shallow blue glass bowl until the nippy morning in November when we cut the last Radiance or Carrousel and place it in a bud vase, there are roses some place in my home. I have yet to discover a rose that isn't worthy of being cut and used for a bouquet. The only ones I have never used are the creepers, and I'm sure that's only because so many other kinds are in bloom when they are.

Large-flowered climbers and ramblers, hybrid teas and hybrid perpetuals, shrub roses and Rugosas all spell richness, when it comes to bouquets. The floribundas and grandifloras are equally good for cutting, especially in hot summer when bloom on the hybrid teas may be rather slim. And if there isn't a vase small enough for a miniature rose, then its flowers can surely be used for a boutonniere or a corsage.

There is as much pleasure for me in having one exquisite Comtesse Vandal or La Jolla or a handsome Sutter's Gold in the silver vase on my desk as there is in having twin vases on the mantelpiece filled with clusters of Dream Girl or, a month later, with Betty Prior roses and Queen Anne's lace. Nothing exceeds the fragrance of three Crimson Glory hybrid teas in a Copenhagen vase, unless it's a satin glass rose bowl full of old-fashioned roses in June. But again Crimson Glory has the advantage, for they can be cut every month from June through October.

There are so many different roses that there are some that can be used appropriately in any kind of vase a person may have. I think that roses, like any other flower, should not be used in a fancy or elaborately decorated vase. After all, the purpose of the vase or bowl is to display the roses, not to compete with them. The only important point in choosing a container is that it be the right height and width for the roses it is to hold. And anyone who grows roses should have three or four small and slender vases of glass, silver or china to hold "just one rose."

Whether one rose or an armful of roses is being cut for bouquets, there are only two times of day when it should be done. That is in the early morning before the sun is high, or in the evening after it has gone down. It's foolish to cut a rose at a time when it will wilt almost immediately instead of opening out fully and lasting several days indoors. Particularly with hybrid teas and hybrid perpetuals, I like to cut them when the first petals are unfurling and watch them open indoors. Even in the hottest summer weather, a rose that has been cut at a favorable time of day and conditioned should last a minimum of three days in water.

A knife and a container of water are the equipment for cutting roses. A knife is the only tool to use, so rosarian J. H. Nicolas told me one winter day years ago, because pruning shears, scissors or a more blunt tool will bruise stem tissues. By all means cut a flower with a stem of decent length. There is, however, sense to the belief that a stem shouldn't be cut with a five-part leaf on it. Either don't cut below a five-part leaf or else leave at least two sets of such leaves behind on the cane. Foliage is needed if the bush is to continue blooming.

Roses should be put into water as fast as they are cut. Attached twin pails with a carrying handle are convenient for anyone who does a great deal of cutting and arranging of flowers to take along into the garden. But any size container with a handle, from the water pail down, that is convenient to carry, will do.

Even though they are placed in water at once, roses should not be arranged in vases as soon as they are brought into the house. To assure that they stay fresh as long as possible, they need conditioning.

Conditioning consists of going over each rose, making a slant-wise cut at the end of the stem and removing thorns along the stem. Both of these tricks allow more surface for the absorption of water. Leaves also should be stripped from the part of the stem that will be under water. Soft green foliage decays when submerged for any length of time.

Having thus prepared each rose that has been cut, plunge

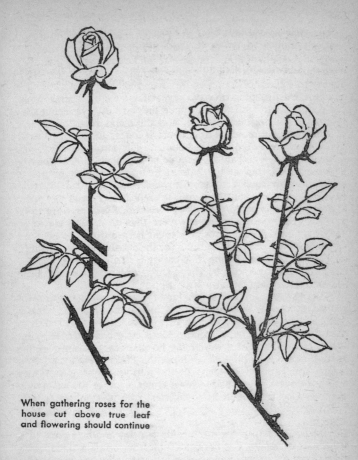

When gathering roses for the
house cut above true leaf
and flowering should continue

them up to their necks in a wide, deep container of water.
This should be placed in a cool, dim place for several hours,
or overnight. I let roses stand for a minimum of four to six
hours before arranging them in vases, and overnight if I plan
to take them in to the office the next morning.

Roses from the florist shop, incidentally, have been conditioned there. But it is best to make a fresh cut, on a slant, at
the end of the stem and to remove foliage that will be below
the water. After you have done this, there is no reason why
florist roses shouldn't be placed at once in containers about
the house.

After roses have been arranged in vases, the placement has

some bearing on how long the flowers remain fresh. Full sunlight, wind or drafts shorten the life of a bouquet. Adequate water is essential at all times, and the amount in the container should be checked daily and replenished if necessary. It is seldom necessary to do more than replenish the water and snip off a drooping blossom, even if a bouquet lasts a week. I'd rather leave roses alone once they are in a vase, but they can, of course, be taken out and the stems recut on a slant after two or three days to encourage longer life.

Roses are not only for bouquets but also to wear. Even wearing only one can be a source of gratification. One may be enough to fasten in the lapel, slip through a belt or pin in the hair, for roses are heavy flowers.

It's not worth cutting a rose to wear if it is done just when dashing out to catch the bus or the train. Roses that are to be worn need conditioning even more than roses that are to go in bouquets. So cut a rose the night before if it is to be worn the next day, or in the morning for the evening, and go through the steps of conditioning it. Wearing a rose on a lapel has one advantage, for it can be slipped into one of those little glass lapel vases that fasten on with a pin.

Some roses are more satisfactory for personal adornment than others. Whatever the class or variety, I would pick it still in the bud stage. It is roses with substance that stand up as boutonnieres or corsages. Most of the hybrid teas are satisfactory, so are many of the floribundas, and some of the polyanthas and climbers. Garnette, Pinkie, Pinocchio and Crimson Rosette are some of the floribundas so satisfactory for corsages that they are grown under glass for the cut-flower trade. Cecile Brunner or sweetheart rose is a polyantha that has been grown for a florist flower as long as it has been known.

Much as I like roses, I prefer wearing a single rose to a corsage of many. For corsages, unless made by a skilled professional florist, are almost certain to be bulky and heavy. But small roses, after conditioning, can be made into a charming nosegay. Three or four buds of grandiflora Queen Elizabeth encircled with rose geranium leaves are pleasing; or one bud of Crimson Glory or Carrousel might be surrounded with double white pinks or sweet alyssum and finished with tiny leaves of ivy. Simple nosegays such as these can be tied with cord or raffia, the ends left to show naturally or covered with aluminum foil.

Corsages of roses are to be worn once; bouquets and arrangements, with all the care in the world, last only about a week. But by going to a little more trouble the fragrance of roses can be captured and kept for years. That means the making of a potpourri, defined as a mixture of spiced flower petals in a jar. There is a special jar for potpourri, known as a rose jar. It was fashionable back in the eighteenth century and persisted well into the nineteenth. Many of the loveliest ones are made of German or English fine bone china. A rose jar is the classic urn shape, with a china sifter that fits into the narrow neck and a matching china lid that slips down over the neck. Two of my favorites are a Canton blue china or crockery one, three inches high, and a Royal Worcester jar about six inches high, with a spray of two pink and red roses and buds.

Recipes for potpourri are often found in old cookbooks, but many women today have figured out their own special recipes. A potpourri starts with the collecting of rose petals in June. Only the most fragrant roses will do. In the era of the potpourri's greatest popularity, the fragrant damask, cabbage and moss roses were cut and their petals dried. Since few gardens today include these scented old roses, it is fortunate that some of the modern ones are very fragrant. Among the modern ones worth cutting for this purpose are the red Gruss an Teplitz, Etoile de Hollande, E. G. Hill, Crimson Glory and Dickson's Red. Among the hybrid perpetual roses, Ulrich Brunner and General Jacqueminot are good for potpourri. A slight perfume does not qualify a rose to be an ingredient of potpourri; it must approach the strong, true rose fragrance.

To retain this fragrance, roses should be cut on a bright, sunny morning following two or three sunny days, after dew has evaporated but before the sun is intense. Roses may be cut at any stage up to fully open, provided they have not been out a couple of days, or so long that they are beginning to fade. The cut roses are brought indoors at once and the petals pulled off. These are spread out in thin layers over a screen, perhaps a window screen not in use, or a rack of cheesecloth. They are placed in a warm but not brightly sunny place that is well ventilated. The petals should be stirred and turned daily until they are dry as chips.

Some people like to fill jars with rose petals only and spices; some like to include other scented blossoms such as lavender, or the scented foliage of rose geranium and lemon verbena. Whether rose petals alone are used, or a mixture with other fragrant flowers and leaves, natural spices are added. These include allspice, cinnamon, cloves, nutmeg, mace and orris root.

A bit of experimenting will soon make a potpourri to the owner's enjoyment. (And lifting the cover on a winter's day brings sweet-scented June to life again.) A good start could be made with about a pint of dried rose petals into which is stirred a tablespoon of mixed ground spices (cloves, nutmeg and cinnamon). This can stand in a covered jar for several weeks, during which time it is stirred occasionally with a wooden spoon. Then, if to a person's liking, it may be divided among rose jars or other appropriate containers; or other spices and scents may be added and stirred until the fragrance is just right.

Rose petals have been used for their fragrance for centuries. In addition to perfume, there was once rose water for washing the hands. There was—and may still be—rose sugar for the table and rose petal candy. During World War II it was discovered in England that rose hips were a rich source of vitamin C, and the hips were made into a preserve or syrup to counteract the lack of oranges and other sources of this important vitamin.

Roses, especially those grown at home, are in so many ways a part of everyday living. Whether home-grown or purchased at the florist shop, they are the flower for all occasions. They are given in celebration of births, graduations and weddings. They congratulate, and they convey sympathy.

The color of the roses given or sent to a person was something to consider back in Victorian days, when the language of flowers was taken seriously enough for books to be published on this subject. According to one of these old books, a dark red rose meant "admiration"; still another book defined the token of a dark red rose as a "confession of love" (and isn't it often so considered today?). A moss rose also was a confession of love. The white rose, alas, meant "too young to love," and a yellow rose told of jealousy. Certainly, by whatever shades of meaning, the rose is the emblem of love.

Nowadays, whatever the color and whether it's one or a dozen, roses as a gift say that one person is thinking of another. And whether the gardener cuts one perfect hybrid tea or an armful of climbers and puts them in a vase, they bespeak in the home of pride and pleasure in growing roses.

Chapter XV

Where Roses Come From

"**O**F MAKING red roses there is no end" is as true today as when it was first written. Each recent decade has brought a generous quota, so generous in fact it almost seems that the originators will run out of appropriate names. Bravo, Redcap, Red Favorite, Red Wonder, Poinsettia, Nocturne, Crimson Glory, Embers, Blaze—on and on they go, interspersed occasionally with a name as literal as Dickson's Red.

Not that the hybridizers have stopped with red roses. They haven't, by any manner of means. These same recent decades have also brought the introduction of fine pinks, stronger yellows, stunning blends and even new tints, such as the coral pink Fashion and cherry coral Vogue.

Most of these new roses—and the majority that will be introduced in the future—have been originated in this country by American hybridists. This was not always the case. Although hybridizing in the United States has gained great momentum in recent years, it did not even begin until about 1900. Strangely enough, although nurseries were established as early as Colonial days, new varieties of roses were for a long time imported from Europe. Some still are and always will be, of course, but the proportion of European to American-bred roses has decreased with every decade of the twentieth century.

One of the most famous roses ever known in this country, the American Beauty, was originated in Europe. It was a hybrid perpetual bred in France and introduced there in 1875 under the name Mme. Ferdinand Jamin. Brought to this country, it was renamed American Beauty.

It is the name, American Beauty, rather than the flower itself which has made this hybrid perpetual such a legend.

Admittedly, it was a beautiful rose in its day. It had long-stemmed, large, many petaled and extremely fragrant flowers of a glowing pink that shaded into carmine. In spite of the name, it was never really a satisfactory rose to grow outdoors in this country, but it could be grown to perfection under glass for a florist's cut flower. And grown under glass it was, everywhere, from about 1900 until 1929. For a few years prior to 1929 it was grown less and less, being supplanted by new and more vigorous growing roses of similar color.

So fixed is the legend that even today people ask the florist for "a dozen American Beauties." So glamorous is the name that florists no longer argue but fill the order with a dozen of their longest-stemmed, most fragrant and glowing red roses. If the florist did still have American Beauty roses, a customer today would pass them by in favor of a newer variety, for we have become accustomed to handsomer roses.

The performance of an American Beauty rosebush in gardens of this country sums up the reasons why hybridizing of roses was undertaken here. It, like so many other European-bred roses, could not be grown well in climate which is so varied and extreme, and was prey for black spot and a host of other troubles. As a result, between 1900 and 1910 a few of the plantsmen in this country began to think about breeding roses to suit the climate and growing conditions here.

As a matter of fact, the first hybrid tea originated in this country had been bred by J. J. Cooke of Baltimore in 1888. He called it Souvenir of Wootton. But it was another twenty years or so before really fine hybrid teas were developed here. Among the trail blazers, in addition to J. J. Cooke, were such rosarians as E. G. Hill of Indiana, Capt. George C. Thomas of California, Dr. W. Van Fleet of Maryland and Fred Howard, also of California. If E. G. Hill were remembered for no other rose than the pink hybrid tea, Mme. Butterfly (1918), that should be sufficient honor for one man. J. J. Cooke is probably best remembered for Radiance (1908). Fred Howard not only originated and named the hybrid tea Los Angeles, but also entered it in the oldest rose test garden in the world, La Roserie de la Haye in Paris, where in 1916 it was the first American-bred rose to win the coveted gold medal.

Nowadays the annual competition at Roserie de la Haye usually offers two gold medals, one for the best rose of European origin, one for the best rose of American origin. But the most coveted award a new rose can receive nowadays is to be voted an All-America Rose Selections winner. Such roses are easily identified because they bear a tag with the insignia and the initials AARS.

Just as credit for proving that roses could be hybridized in this country goes to several persons rather than to any one person, so, too, does credit for the formation of the All-America Rose Selections Committee. Their first rose test garden was established in 1938, and now there are twenty-three test gardens across the country. They have been established in every sort of climate.

New varieties of roses are entered in the annual AARS trials by a hybridist or a nursery. Bushes must be supplied to each of the twenty-three test gardens and are planted with a code number, not a name. These roses are observed and their performance noted by competent judges several times during the growing season for two years. The scoring is likely to vary from one test garden to another, chiefly because of climate. Certain it is that few of the candidates become AARS roses at the end of the two-year testing period.

The first AARS awards were announced in 1940. This announcement is made in June of each year for the succeeding year, and in fall and the following spring bushes are available from the majority of rose nurserymen (an adequate supply is one of the conditions of entering the AARS competition).

AARS winners, for the most part, are varieties that perform well in all regions of the country. Only rarely, as in 1944 with hybrid tea Fred Edmunds and in 1948 with climber High Noon, is a sectional recommendation made (these two do best in mild climate).

While we can be certain that an All-America Rose Selections winner will be a fine plant, a new variety isn't necessarily damned because it wasn't entered by its originator or didn't win an award. Carrousel, the red grandiflora, is only one example of a fine rose that grows everywhere but does not carry an AARS tag. However, a new rose that sounds appealing but doesn't bear an AARS tag, calls for more investigation than one that does, before I spend my money for a plant.

Many fine new roses still come from Europe. There is Peace, originated by Francis Meilland in France and, more recently, Confidence from the same hybridizer. Also from France, but originated by C. Mallerin, are the white Blanche Mallerin and the yellow Lowell Thomas. World's Fair came from Wilhelm Kordes in Germany, Irene of Denmark from Svend Poulsen in Copenhagen, Golden Scepter from Verschuren-Pechtold in Holland and Baby Gold Star from Pedro Dot in Spain.

Most of today's American hybridizers carry on their work on the West Coast, primarily in California. Although the number probably is greater there, a few are scattered throughout the rest of the country.

Wherever the hybridizer develops a new variety of rose,

whether in this country or in Europe, it is now patented before it is released for propagation and sale. The Plant Patent Act has been in effect since 1930, and the first rose to be patented was the climber New Dawn.

Any new variety of rose may be patented, so long as the person who applies for the patent proves that it is, in some way, different from existing varieties. A patent is no guarantee of beauty, vigor or performance. The chief purpose of the patent is to protect the originator of the rose and to protect the variety. For in order to propagate additional bushes of a patented rose, such as Carrousel or Peace or Circus or Sutter's Gold, it is essential to have a license from the owner of the patent. The right to propagate is leased out to wholesale rose growers on a royalty basis.

A patent, therefore, demolishes any inclinations an amateur gardener may have of growing additional plants from the one he has planted in his garden. Legally he cannot do so. And, practically, an amateur should not attempt to grow rosebushes from scratch.

The propagation (or the multiplication) of rosebushes is accomplished by a special process known as budding. In its greatest simplification, this means the insertion of a bud of a specified variety, such as hybrid tea First Love, into an opening in the bark of a different stock. This rootstock will be some kind of rose—and different wholesale growers have their preferences—that is exceptionally hardy and vigorous. This means a nurseryman must grow acres of rootstock plants, as well as acres of plants for budwood, and still have acres of budded roses growing on to a salable size. The tops of the rootstock plants are cut off at ground level at the most favorable time of year for budding, and this work is done by skilled, trained labor.

There is considerably more to growing rosebushes of good quality on a wholesale basis than this. The wholesale grower who is tending thousands of plants must combat black spot, thrips and other insects and diseases. He must water and fertilize even more religiously than does the amateur gardener.

The growing of rosebushes on a wholesale scale, therefore, has become a business in areas of favorable soil and climate. The home office of one of the most widely known rose nurseries, Jackson & Perkins, is located in Newark, New York, which is not far from Lake Ontario. Jackson & Perkins not only test roses, but also do considerable growing of roses in northwestern New York State. However, by far the greatest number of rosebushes sold by this firm every year are grown on their acreage in California and Arizona. There are other wholesale rose-growing areas in the East and the Midwest, but

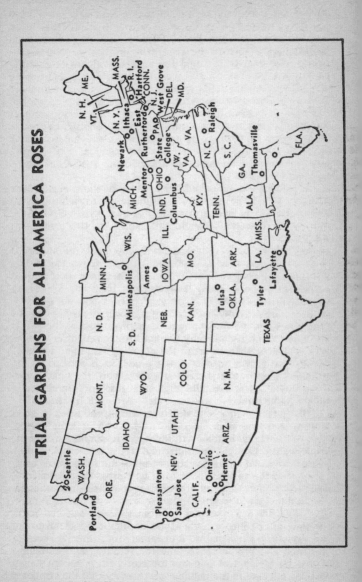

TRIAL GARDENS FOR ALL-AMERICA ROSES

these are comparatively small. No matter where a rosebush is purchased, the chances are good that it was budded and grown in either California or the vicinity of Tyler, Texas.

Again, there is no such thing as a bargain rose. A good rose is worth every cent that is paid for it. New varieties of roses, including AARS winners, average $2.50 to $3 each. (Generally there is a slight saving if three, six or a dozen are purchased—perhaps thirty cents on a bush.) Older varieties of roses average $1.35 to $2 each.

At these prices, the bush unquestionably should be two years old and field-grown. Not all two-year-old field-grown bushes, even of the same variety, are identical. So when plants are dug and brought into the packing shed, they are sorted and graded. A No. 1 grade hybrid tea bush, which sells at the prices mentioned, should have three or more eighteen-inch canes. (The canes are usually pruned back to eight inches by the nurseryman before shipping.) A No. 1½ hybrid tea has three canes twelve inches long; a No. 2 has two canes or more.

Bushes other than No. 1 grade will grow and with special care could, in less than a year, equal the performance of a No. 1 bush which has been neglected. The lesser grades of roses sell for proportionately less money. A bargain offer such as eight hybrid teas for $2.95 probably means that the plants have been discarded by a greenhouse grower, who has been cutting roses for the florist trade from these bushes for two years. There is no room in my garden for such plants.

As to whether there is room for anything less than a two-year-old, field-grown bush of No. 1 grade, each person must decide for himself. It's the old story of "you get what you pay for." The current retail price of a rosebush purchased from a reliable grower is not too much. After all, it takes two years of understanding and skilled care to produce a good rosebush. And the slight increase in cost for a brand-new variety is certainly justified. It takes, at a minimum, eight years from the time the hybridist makes his first cross, with the dream rose only a figment in his mind, until that rose can be placed on the market. And for every cross that becomes a new rose, name and all, thousands of other crosses are grown, studied and discarded.

It is only when a rose plant has finally been selected for marketing, after being tested and judged, that the hybridist or nurseryman gives it a name. Remember, too, that the years of research and production behind the selection and naming of a rose have been too long and too costly for a nurseryman to risk introducing to the public a new variety that they might not like or that will not add luster to his nursery.

The name finally given to a rose replaces the number under which it has been growing. A rose always has its name stamped on the package which encloses it, or on a tag twisted around a cane. I like to know the rosebushes in my garden by name and to be able to tell any visitors who ask about one they admire: "That's Sutter's Gold," or "La Jolla" or "President Eisenhower." So I make a rough plan for each rose bed with check marks and numbers to indicate the bushes planted, and then down one side of the page I list the numbers, followed by variety. It's easy to forget which rose is which from one spring to the next, and knowing roses by name adds a great deal of pleasure to growing them.

It hardly seems as though there could be handsomer or finer roses for gardens than Sutter's Gold, La Jolla, President Eisenhower and a couple dozen more new—and old—varieties. But I am certain that in ten years or so, more of the new varieties of roses will have more fragrance than have many modern ones today. I am also certain that more varieties will not only have greater disease resistance but also be practically disease-proof.

Although variety Helen Traubel is spoken of as having a spicy fragrance, Katherine T. Marshall a fruity one, and Pink Dawn as being just plain sweet, many people have commented on either lack of fragrance or less intense fragrance in many varieties introduced in the last twenty years or so. As indication of their awareness, some of the hybridists have stated that they will include more fragrance among their goals. As an aid to the pursuit of fragrance in future varieties, a gift of money was given to the American Rose Foundation in 1955 to sponsor research on the genetics of fragrance. This gift was inaugurated by Dr. James Alexander Gamble of Maryland, who pledged to duplicate his initial sum of $1,000 each year of his life.

Announcement of this gift was made by the American Rose Society, a clearing house for anyone, amateur or professional, who grows roses or is interested in them. Membership is open to anyone who wishes to join, for the sum of $4.50 annually. Headquarters of the American Rose Society are at 4048 Roselea Place, Columbus 14, Ohio. Its resources include a library and display and test gardens, and members receive not only the copy of the annual yearbook but also other publications throughout the year.

Anyone who grows roses shares a broad fellowship, and one that increases every time a new homeowner plants his first rosebush. It has become easier today for the rankest novice to have lavish success with the first bushes that he plants.

Roses are changing as much during the twentieth century as is any other facet of everyday living. During the first half of the twentieth century, the hybrid tea rose has reigned supreme. The hybrid tea will always be with us—too many of them are too beautiful not to be maintained. But the second half of the twentieth century brings two modern groups—floribunda and grandiflora—surging to the fore.

A super class of rose may lie ahead, as yet not developed and perhaps not even thought of, although I would be the last person to underestimate one or two of our most skilled hybridizers. This much is certain: Roses will be grown and tended lovingly a hundred years from now, and on through the ages, just as they have been through the ages behind us.

All-America Rose Selections Award Winners
1940—1965

Year	Name	Group	Color
1965	Camelot	Grandiflora	Coral pink
	Mister Lincoln	Hybrid Tea	Deep, velvety red
1964	Granada	Hybrid Tea	Reds and yellow
	Saratoga	Floribunda	White
1963	Royal Highness	Hybrid Tea	Light pink
	Tropicana	Hybrid Tea	Orange red
1962	Christian Dior	Hybrid Tea	Bright crimson
	Golden Slippers	Floribunda	Gold and orange
	John S. Armstrong	Grandiflora	Dark red
	King's Ransom	Hybrid Tea	Chrome yellow
1961	Duet	Hybrid Tea	Pink bicolor
	Pink Parfait	Grandiflora	Light pink
1960	Garden Party	Hybrid Tea	White, tinged with pink
	Fire King	Floribunda	Vermilion
	Saraband	Floribunda	Scarlet orange
1959	Starfire	Grandiflora	Cherry red
	Ivory Fashion	Floribunda	Ivory white
1958	Fusillier	Floribunda	Orange red
	Gold Cup	Floribunda	Yellow
	White Knight	Hybrid Tea	White
1957	Golden Showers	Climber	Yellow
	White Bouquet	Floribunda	White
1956	Circus	Floribunda	Multicolor
1955	Tiffany	Hybrid Tea	Bicolor: yellow, pink
	Jiminy Cricket	Floribunda	Coral orange
	Queen Elizabeth	Grandiflora	Delicate pink

Year	Name	Group	Color
1954	Lilibet	Floribunda	Clear pink
	Mojave	Hybrid Tea	Apricot orange
1953	Chrysler Imperial	Hybrid Tea	Crimson
	Ma Perkins	Floribunda	Coral shell-pink
1952	Fred Howard	Hybrid Tea	Yellow, penciled pink
	Vogue	Floribunda	Cherry coral
	Helen Traubel	Hybrid Tea	Apricot pink
1950	Fashion	Floribunda	Coral pink
	Mission Bells	Hybrid Tea	Salmon
	Capistrano	Hybrid Tea	Pink
	Sutter's Gold	Hybrid Tea	Golden yellow
1949	Forty-Niner	Hybrid Tea	Bicolor: red, yellow
	Tallyho	Hybrid Tea	Two-tone pink
1948	Diamond Jubilee	Hybrid Tea	Buff
	High Noon*	Climber	Yellow
	Nocturne	Hybrid Tea	Dark red
	Pinkie	Polyantha	Light rose-pink
	San Fernando	Hybrid Tea	Currant red
	Taffeta	Hybrid Tea	Two-tone pink yellow
1947	Rubaiyat	Hybrid Tea	Cerise
1946	Peace	Hybrid Tea	Pale gold
1945	Floradora	Floribunda	Salmon rose
	Horace McFarland	Hybrid Tea	Buff pink
	Mirandy	Hybrid Tea	Crimson
1944	Fred Edmunds*	Hybrid Tea	Apricot
	Katherine T. Marshall	Hybrid Tea	Deep pink
	Lowell Thomas	Hybrid Tea	Butter yellow
	Mme. Chiang Kai-shek	Hybrid Tea	Light yellow
	Mme. Marie Curie	Hybrid Tea	Golden yellow
1943	Grande Duchess Charlotte	Hybrid Tea	Wine red
	Mary Margaret McBride	Hybrid Tea	Rose pink
1942	Heart's Desire	Hybrid Tea	Deep rose-red
1941	Charlotte Armstrong	Hybrid Tea	Cerise
	Apricot Queen	Hybrid Tea	Apricot
	California	Hybrid Tea	Golden yellow
1940	Dickson's Red	Hybrid Tea	Scarlet
	Flash	Climber	Oriental red
	The Chief	Hybrid Tea	Salmon red
	World's Fair	Floribunda	Deep red

* Denotes sectional recommendation.

Summary of Rose Care

INNUMERABLE roses survive and flower even if they are neglected. But in order to obtain the greatest pleasure from roses, there is a round of chores scattered throughout the year. The timing below is for the temperate states, a wide belt across the country from the East Coast to the Rocky Mountains, and extending slightly north of New York City in the east and as far south as Kansas City in the midwest. For other specific climatic areas, the timing should be adjusted to the arrival of spring and planting weather and to the progress of the seasons.

March   Plant new rosebushes as soon as the ground is workable.

        Prune all roses, except the ramblers, before leaves open. "Prune when forsythia blooms."

April   Fertilize by sprinkling a 5-10-5 fertilizer in a circle around each plant. Then cultivate the soil with a hoe or long-handled cultivator.

        Start the weekly schedule of spraying if necessary.

May   Cultivate to keep down weeds.

        Spray weekly.

        Edge beds or borders.

June	Fertilize when bloom starts.
	Cultivate after a rain. Then mulch for the summer to keep down weeds and conserve moisture in the soil.
	Cut roses for bouquets with a knife in the morning or evening.
	Continue to spray every week hybrid teas and any other roses that require it.
	Snip off dead flowers.
July	Continue to spray weekly.
	Fertilize lightly between July 1-15.
	Prune ramblers and large-flowered climbers.
	Continue to cut off dead flowers.
	Hand-pick Japanese beetles.
August September October	Continue to spray weekly; cut off dead flowers.
November December	Add winter coverings after the ground freezes.

10 Don'ts

A ROSE can be the most satisfactory plant in the garden, and the easiest to grow. And planting a rosebush can be the fastest road to obtaining color there. Just to make certain that this comes true, the following precautions are suggested to the novice:

1. Don't look for bargain roses. A No. 1 grade, two-year-old field-grown bush is worth the modest price a reliable local or mail-order nursery asks.

2. Don't buy and plant more rosebushes than there will be time and energy to care for.

3. Don't buy only hybrid teas—there are other fine classes of roses—if there isn't time to spray them every week during the growing season.

4. Don't skimp on soil preparation.

5. Don't let bushes, especially their roots, dry out before or during planting.

6. Don't neglect the spray schedule during the growing season.

7. Don't water in the late afternoon or evening, and don't spray in the evening (page 67).

8. Don't sprinkle rosebushes. Soak the soil instead of using a sprinkler or other means of overhead watering.

9. Don't let seed pods form; snip off faded blossoms.

10. Don't be afraid to prune hybrid tea roses (correct pruning every spring is essential to good bloom).

Rose Gardens Open
to the Public

CATALOGUES are inspiration enough to try a new or different variety of rose, but it is always a good idea for the gardener to go out and see the real thing. Listed below are public and private gardens across the country where people can check on newer roses or admire old favorites. Although most of the private collections can be seen without an appointment, it would be advisable for visitors to check in advance. And while roses grow in every state of the union, it has not been possible to list a specific garden for each of the forty-eight.

Alabama	Birmingham: Avondale Park
Arizona	Phoenix: Valley Garden Center
	Tempe: Rose garden of Dr. J. E. Zimmerman, 304 East Fifteenth Street
	Tombstone: Rose Tree Inn
	Tucson: Memorial Rose Garden, Randolph Way
California	Berkeley: Municipal Rose Garden
	La Canada: Descanso Gardens (historic and modern roses)
	Los Angeles: Exposition Park
	Oakland: Linda Vista Park
	Pasadena: Rose Bowl
	Riverside: White Park
	Sacramento: Municipal Rose Garden
	San Jose: Municipal Rose Garden
	Santa Barbara: Memorial Rose Garden

Colorado   Denver: Arboretum and Rose Garden; Arlighton, Berkeley, Cheesman and Washington Parks; Montclair and Sixth Avenue Parkways
Pueblo: Mineral Palace Park

Connecticut   Ansonia: Garden of Dr. George A. Comstock, 217 Wakelee Avenue
Hartford: Elizabeth Park
New Haven: Pardee Rose Garden, East Rock Park
Norwich: Memorial Rose Garden
Waterbury: Hamilton Park

Delaware   Wilmington: Brandywine Park; Jasper Crane Rose Garden

District of Columbia   Franciscan Monastery; National Rose Garden, Potomac Park

Florida   Jacksonville: Garden Center

Georgia   Albany: Municipal Park
Atlanta: Municipal Park; Druid Hills Municipal Rose Garden
Thomasville: Municipal Park
Waycross: Municipal Rose Garden

Idaho   Boise: Municipal Rose Garden
Caldwell: Municipal Rose Garden
Nampa: Lakeview Park
North Lewiston: Lewiston Memorial Park
Pocatello: Rotary Rose Garden

Illinois   Aurora: Phillip's Park
Chicago: Humboldt Park; Washington Park
East St. Louis: Rose Garden
Evanston: Merrick Park
Highland Park: Memorial Rose Garden; Ravinia Park
Lisle: Morton Arboretum
Mundelein: "Rosebrae," estate of C. Eugene Pfister (temporarily closed)
Ravinia: Rose Garden, Roger Williams Avenue
Rockford: Rockford Park District Rose Garden
Silvis: Municipal Rose Garden

Indiana   Fort Wayne: Municipal Rose Garden; Lakeside Park

Michigan City: Persian Rose Garden, International Friendship Gardens

Richmond: E. Gurney Hill Memorial Garden, Glen Miller Park

Iowa   Ames: Many streets bordered with roses

Davenport: Municipal Park

Des Moines: Greenwood Park

Indianola: Buxton Park

Sioux City: Municipal Rose Garden

Kansas   Lawrence: Municipal Rose Garden

Manhattan: Rose Garden, campus of Kansas State College; Kiwanis Rose Garden, Municipal Park

Salina: Oakdale Park

Topeka: Reinisch Rose Garden, Gage Park

Kentucky   Louisville: Reservoir Park

Louisiana   New Orleans: City Park

Maine   Portland: Municipal Rose Garden

South Portland: Rose garden of Mr. and Mrs. Rupert Neily, 48 Drew Road

Maryland   Baltimore: Baltimore Museum of Art; Druid Hill Park

Massa-chusetts   Andover: Garden of Mr. and Mrs. Charles W. Arnold

Boston: Franklin Park; Fenway Park

Falmouth: Rose garden of Sumner C. Burgess

Greenwood: Rose garden of George H. Moncrieff, 14 Crystal Street

Holyoke: Municipal Rose Garden

Jamaica Plain: Arnold Arboretum

Marblehead: Rose garden of Mrs. Francis B. Crowninshield

Quincy: York rosebush, John Quincy Adams House—believed to have been planted by President John Adams' wife in 1788

Quissett: Rose garden of Mr. and Mrs. Edwin S. Webster

Springfield: Forest Park

Westport: "Old Brook Farm," home of William H. Tillson

Michigan   East Lansing: Michigan State College

Jackson: Ella Sharp Memorial Park

Lake Odessa: Rose garden of Thomas Johnson

Lansing: Cooley Gardens

Minnesota Minneapolis: Lyndale Park

South Minneapolis: Municipal Rose Garden

Mississippi Biloxi: Formal Rose Garden, Veterans' Administration Hospital

Jackson: Municipal Rose Garden, Livingston Park

Long Beach: Municipal Gardens

Missouri Independence: Glendale Rose Garden

Kansas City: Jacob L. Loose Rose Garden, Memorial Park

St. Louis: Rose plantings along highways entering city; Jewel Box Rose Garden; Missouri Botanical Garden (Shaw's Garden)

Montana Lewistown: Municipal Rose Garden

Missoula: Sunset Park

Nebraska Lincoln: Antelope Park; University of Nebraska Formal Rose Garden

Omaha: Rose Garden, Florence Home for the Aged

New Hampshire Concord: Rose garden of Frank J. Sulloway

New Jersey Elizabeth: Mattano Park

Essex County: Weequahic Park

Glen Ridge: Test garden of Dr. Cynthia Westcott, 96 Essex Avenue

Summit: Watchung stables—multiflora roses on paddock fences

New Mexico Albuquerque: Municipal Garden

New York Auburn: Municipal Rose Garden

Buffalo: Humboldt Park

Farmingdale: Long Island Agricultural and Technical Institute

Middletown: State Hospital Rose Garden

Newark: Jackson & Perkins Company Rose Garden

New Rochelle: Hudson Park

New York City: Cranford Rose Garden, Brooklyn Botanic Garden; New York Botanical Garden, Bronx Park; Queens

Botanical Garden, Flushing; United Nations Rose Garden, Manhattan

Niagara Falls: Hyde Park

Rochester: Highland Park; Maplewood Park

Syracuse: Dr. E. M. Mills Rose Garden, Thornden Park

Yonkers: Boyce Thompson Institute Rose Garden

North Carolina
Charlotte: Municipal Rose Garden; Sunnyside Rose Garden

High Point: High Point, Thomasville & Denton Railroad Company rose gardens

Raleigh: North Carolina State College rose garden (for testing mainly); Municipal Rose Garden

North Dakota
Fargo: Rose garden of Dr. Charles Heilman, 49 Eighteenth Avenue North

Ohio
Barberton: J. E. White Nursery

Bay Village: City of Bay Village

Cleveland: Shaker Heights Community Rose Garden; Park of Roses

Columbus: Ohio State University test gardens; Kingwood Center

Elyria: Garden of Dr. John P. Rankin

Kirtland Hills: Holden Arboretum

Lorain: Municipal Rose Garden

Mentor: Formal Rose Garden, Melvin E. Wyant Nursery; Paul R. Bosley Nursery; Joseph J. Kern Rose Nursery

Rocky River: Municipal Rose Garden

Toledo: Ottawa Park

Oklahoma
Enid: Municipal Rose Garden

Oklahoma City: Will Rogers Park

Tulsa: Rose Garden

Woodward: Rose Garden

Oregon
Eugene: Rose Society garden

Portland, "the Rose City": Washington Park; Royal Rosarian Rose Garden; Capt. George C. Thomas Jr. Memorial Garden; U. S. Veterans' Hospital informal rose garden; Lewis and Clark College Memorial Rose Garden; Peninsula Park Sunken Rose Garden; roses growing along the streets

Pennsylvania   Allentown: Malcolm W. Gross Memorial
      Rose Garden
Bethlehem: Wise Side Park
Conshohocken: Zeigler's Rose Garden
Elizabethtown: Masonic Home Rose Garden
Harrisburg: "Breeze Hill," estate of the late
      Dr. J. Horace McFarland; Municipal
      Rose Garden
Hershey: Rose Garden
Kennett Square: Longwood Gardens
McKeesport: Renziehausen Park Arboretum
Philadelphia: Mellon Park Rose Gardens
Pottstown: Municipal Rose Garden
Reading: Rose Garden
Sewickley: Rose garden of Mrs. J. Lee
      Plummer Jr., Two Beaver Road
York: City Council's Formal Display Gar-
      den

Rhode   Little Compton: Brownell Rose Research
Island   Gardens
Providence: Roger Williams Park

South   Columbia: Valley Park
Carolina   Orangeburg: Edisto Gardens
Sumter: Edmonds Memorial Rose Garden

South
Dakota   Sioux Falls: State Rose Garden

Tennessee   Chattanooga: Warner Park
Memphis: Municipal Rose Garden

Texas   Amarillo: Memorial Park Rose Garden
College Station: Agricultural and Mechani-
      cal College of Texas Rose Garden
Dallas: Oak Cliff Park
El Paso: Municipal Rose Garden
Fort Worth: Rotary Park Botanic Gardens
Houston: Hermann Park
Lubbock: Municipal Rose Garden
Port Arthur: Municipal Rose Garden
Tyler: Municipal Rose Garden; Courthouse
      plantings

Utah   Provo: Municipal Rose Garden
Salt Lake City: Municipal Rose Gardens;
      Liberty Park

Vermont	Burlington: Rose gardens of John E. Booth, 86 Williams Street; J. W. Goss, Ledge Road; Dr. Peter P. Lawlor, Ledge Road; and O. T. Sullivan, 61 North Willard Street
	Essex Junction: Rose garden of H. K. Drury, Pleasant Street
Virginia	Arlington: Memorial Planting
	Blacksburg: Experimental Rose Plots, Virginia Polytechnic Institute; Rose garden of the Virginia Agricultural Experiment Station
	Jamestown: English Rose Garden, church grounds
	Richmond: Rose Test Garden
	Roanoke: Elmwood Park
	Norfolk: Lafayette Park
Washington	Aberdeen: Samuel Benn Park
	Bellingham: Fairhaven Park
	Chehalis: Municipal Rose Garden
	Seattle: Rose Garden
	Tacoma: Point Defiance Park; Lincoln Park; McKinley Park
West Virginia	Huntington: Ritter Park
Wisconsin	Hales Corners: Whitnall Park Botanical Gardens
	Kenosha: Lincoln Park
Wyoming	Lovell: Rose garden of Dr. W. W. Horsley

Glossary

M ANY WORDS, used glibly by a gardener of some years' standing, or in a nursery catalogue, are baffling to the newcomer. More often than not, however, the words have not basically changed from their original meaning, but are used in a different yet apt way gardenwise. Following are words used in this book that generally have a specific application to the growing of roses:

Balled and burlaped (or b&b)—referring to a plant that has been dug with a ball of soil around its roots, and with roots and soil wrapped in burlap and tied. Roses are seldom, if ever, purchased balled and burlaped.

Balling—the inability of a rose to open completely because of the presence in the flower of insects or disease. Buds open part way only, petals seem stuck together, and the flower remains round or ball-shaped.

Bare root—referring to a woody plant such as a rose that is dug when dormant with no attempt to keep roots covered with soil.

Bed—a level piece of ground in which plants are set out in mass.

Border—a piece of ground longer than it is wide and perhaps following a wall, fence, driveway or shrubs for background.

Bud—an undeveloped leaf, flower or shoot protruding from the stem of a plant.
Specifically in roses, to insert a bud of a specified variety into an opening in the bark of a different stock.

Calyx—The outer circle of a flower, composed of sepals, which are green in a rose.

Cane—the stem of a rose, typically covered with thin bark, green or brown, and with few or many thorns.

Cultivate—to loosen the soil between plants by means of a hoe or cultivator, thus removing weeds and breaking up the soil into fine particles.

Disbud—the removal of the small side buds beneath the large terminal bud to permit the fullest development of the terminal one.

Dormant—to be in the state of inactive growth, or resting; specifically in a rose, to be in the state of lacking flowers and foliage during winter.

Dust—to sprinkle an insecticide or fungicide from a container over the parts of a plant infected with disease or insects.

Everblooming—the successive production of flowers throughout summer and fall until frost.

Eye—an undeveloped bud, either leaf or flower.

Hardy—capable of living through winter without special protection.

Hill up—to heap soil around the stems of a rose bush, in a small hill.

Hip—the ripened fruit of a rose, containing seed.

Hybrid—a plant resulting from the crossing of two different plants of the same species, and differing markedly from either of its parents.

Lateral—a short side stem with leaves and flowers growing out from a main branch.

Mulch—clean material spread over the soil between plants to protect their roots from heat, cold or drought. Saves watering and cultivating.

Peg—to fasten the long stem of a climber or shrub rose with a clothespin, if to soil, or with some other device, if to a wall or hard surface.

Propagate—to increase or multiply the number of plants.

Remontant—periodic repeat bloom during summer and fall typical of certain types and varieties of roses after their first display in June.

Roses—the following types or classes are discussed:

CLIMBER—a rose that produces long, flexible canes that require support to grow upright. The three main subdivisions are climbing hybrid teas, large-flowered climbers, and ramblers.

FLORIBUNDA—a bush rose that may grow two to four feet tall, according to variety, and is characterized by clusters of large single or double flowers produced from June until autumn frost.

GRANDIFLORA—a bush rose, growing four to six feet tall, characterized by large flowers borne singly or in clusters on stems long enough for cutting. Free flowering all summer.

HYBRID PERPETUAL—a strong-growing bush characterized by sturdy, vertical stems. Flowers in June; usually remontant thereafter.

HYBRID TEA—bush roses averaging three feet tall, characterized by handsome bloom, produced from May or June, and thereafter regularly until autumn frost. A few varieties single; the majority, double flowers in a full range of rose colors.

MINIATURE—small bushes, six to twelve inches tall, with foliage and flowers in scale to height. Roses less than an inch across.

POLYANTHA—a bush rose, much branched, spreading and approximately two feet tall. Clusters of small blossoms, produced continuously.

RAMBLER—a climbing rose characterized by clusters of small blossoms produced only once a year, in June or July.

SHRUB—a four- to six-foot, many-stemmed rosebush that may be upright, fountain- or mound-shaped in habit of growth. Mostly single flowers, often small, and appearing only once a year.

TRAILER—a long-stemmed rose whose tendency is to grow over the ground, and which is therefore difficult to train upward against a support as may be done with true climbers.

TREE (OR STANDARD)—a single two- to four-foot stem topped with a crown of foliage or flowers that may be hybrid tea, floribunda or grandiflora.

Species—a group of plants that possess in common one or more distinctive and constant characteristics.

Specimen—a plant grown by itself for effective display.

Sport—a flower that appears spontaneously and varies in some characteristic from the plant that produced it.

Spray—to cover parts of a plant infected with insects or disease with a suitable chemical diluted in water.

Stake—to support a plant by tying its stem to a length of wood anchored in the ground alongside.

Stock—the rooted portion of a plant in which a bud is inserted to form a new plant.

Sucker—a stem of underground origin characterized by rapid and vertical growth and differing somewhat from other stems of the plant.

Variety—a plant within a species, but having some identifying characteristic of its own, perhaps color.

Introducing
9 Bantam Gothic Novels

Haunted houses, sinister plots, dread forces of evil, mysterious deaths, obsessive love and revenge. All this and more in Bantam's new Gothic Novel Series. Written by some of the world's foremost Gothic writers, here are nine spellbinding tales not to be missed.

The romantic world of
EMILIE LORING

Women of all ages are falling under the enchanting spell that famous author Emilie Loring weaves in her novels. She has filled each book with strong drama, making each story a breathtaking reading experience. Enter the romantic world of Emilie Loring. Once you have finished one book by her, you are bound to want to read all of her others.

- ☐ 1 FOR ALL YOUR LIFE
- ☐ 2 WHAT THEN IS LOVE
- ☐ 3 I TAKE THIS MAN
- ☐ 4 MY DEAREST LOVE
- ☐ 5 LOOK TO THE STARS
- ☐ 6 BEHIND THE CLOUD
- ☐ 7 THE SHADOW OF SUSPICION
- ☐ 8 WITH THIS RING
- ☐ 9 BEYOND THE SOUND OF GUNS
- ☐ 10 HOW CAN THE HEART FORGET
- ☐ 11 TO LOVE AND TO HONOR
- ☐ 12 LOVE CAME LAUGHING BY
- ☐ 13 I HEAR ADVENTURE CALLING
- ☐ 14 THROW WIDE THE DOOR
- ☐ 15 BECKONING TRAILS
- ☐ 16 BRIGHT SKIES
- ☐ 17 THERE IS ALWAYS LOVE
- ☐ 18 STARS IN YOUR EYES
- ☐ 19 KEEPERS OF THE FAITH
- ☐ 20 WHERE BEAUTY DWELLS

50¢ each—available wherever paperbacks are sold, or write

Bantam Books, Inc., Dept. EL, Room 607, 271 Madison Ave., N. Y., N. Y. 10016.

Please send me the titles I have checked.

Name_____

Address_____

City_____State_____Zip Code_____

(Please send check or money order. No currency or C.O.D.'s. Add 10¢ per book on orders of less than 5 books to cover the cost of postage and handling.) Allow two to three weeks for delivery. EL 12/66

FREE CATALOG
of over 650 Bantam Books

• All The New Releases • Best-Selling Authors • Chilling Mysteries • Thundering Westerns • Startling Science-Fiction • Gripping Novels • Anthologies • Dramas • Reference Books • More.

BANTAM BOOKS
—
CURRENT CATALOG

This fascinating catalog of Bantam Books contains a complete list of paper-bound editions of best-selling books originally priced from $2.00 to $7.00. Yours now in Bantam editions for just 35¢ to $1.45. Here is your opportunity to read the best-sellers you've missed, and add to your private library at huge savings. The catalog is free! Send for yours today.

Ready for Mailing Now
Send for your FREE copy today